Susan Hawthorne, polyglot scholar and pontless women across the ages! The talk's torrenti ltural crossovers dizzying. Expect the unexpecte g and prayer, and Palaeolithic Lupa across the tabl

—Judith Rodriguez AM

Lupa and Lamb begins with a descent into the unknown in the cave of the Sibilla Cumana, and then swirling through stars and constellations. Susan Hawthorne encompasses "la grande bellezza" ("sweet Roma where else would you want to be?"), leading us to the "emotional leap into other realms / a transit out of time into timelessness" "to find the unfound and unfindable".

—Marina Morbiducci, Professor of English Language and Translation, Sapienza University, Rome

Who'd have thought that erudition could be so exotic, erotic and dazzlingly entertaining? In this triumphantly inventive excursion into feminist revisionism, Hawthorne is fully mistress of language and genre as she brings her Roman women into view in the diverse roles – lover, poet, prostitute, martyr – and the sometimes dark fates that await them as living instances of she-wolf and lamb.

—Jennifer Strauss AM

This vibrant collection of lyric poetry exhumes female ardour from among old male traditions. It asks us again and again why we are not open to the emotional rhythms that come down to us from the Aegean and from Rome: but also from mythic vibrations that were awake even far earlier. These poems ask us to wake up and live.

—Chris Wallace-Crabbe AM

Reading *Lupa and Lamb*, I was transported back to a time of wondering and wandering. Where bones and museum artefacts lose their dryness, become fully fleshed and whisper their stories intimately in your ear. Here the full pagan glory of Italy meets the inquisitive and absorbing gaze of Australian poet Susan Hawthorne's eye. Heart-breaking, sensual and unexpectedly funny.

—Kavisha Mazzella, singer and songwriter

Combining erudition with emotion and eroticism, intellect with imagination, Susan Hawthorne weaves women's forgotten history into a magic web of remembering and re-imagining. With her playful juxtapositions of words, names, times, places and species, she shows there is freedom in not forgetting, and that the world could have been – can be – different.

—Robyn Arianrhod, author of *Seduced by Logic*

Susan Hawthorne has created a wonderfully rich imaginative poetic tapestry, weaving together fragments of lost and found memories, mythology, archaeology, ancient languages and modern cosmology. An erudite feminist, once again thought provoking and fun.

— Meryl Waugh, PhD (Astrophysics), University of Melbourne

Susan Hawthorne's words honour ancient inspirations, revive and celebrate the past and transport the reader to new horizons.

— Powhiri Wharemarama Rika-Heke, Learning Leader, Social Sciences, Alfriston College

Lupa and Lamb which follows the root and transformation of languages through their own transmigration, is more than poetry, more than history, more than a mnemonic tool which can assist the initiated in re-engaging with women-centred psychology. At the core of *Lupa and Lamb* is a treatise in confronting and understanding the self in the present, through a panoramic prism of the mythical past.

— Lella Cariddi, poet, artist, curator

Reading *Lupa and Lamb* is not like opening Pandora's box. The treasures released: poetry that redeems the voices and torn whispers of millennia of women, give only delight. Playful Curatrix eases us through ancient languages, myths and the intricate details of love and lust. Always we are reminded that *poiēsis* is fabrication, creation and re-making; this is how the past can be found and reworked into divine gifts.

— Lyn Hatherly, author of *Acts of Abrasion* and *Sappho's Sweetbitter Songs*

… a complicated and dense book. Wonderfully written and so much depth in it.

— Robyn Rowland AO, author of *Seasons of Doubt and Burning*

Inspired by her residency at the Whiting Studio in Rome, Susan Hawthorne's *Lupa and Lamb* explores the mysteries of ancient sites and treasures in Rome and nearby countries, linking the past with the present, and collecting hidden treasures the archaeologists have missed. Poems, plays and 'lost texts' of women through the ages are presented in words and imagery that offer sensual and intellectual delights. This is 'translation' in its widest sense – a collection to be treasured and reread.

— Elaine Lewis, author of *Left Bank Waltz*

Susan Hawthorne has created a lovely, lively combination of learning, intellect, passion and fun in *Lupa and Lamb*. Both profound and playful, these poems entertain, uplift and inform. Curatrix's offering at the beginning and the end are a particular delight.

— Pat Rosier, author of *Where the Heart Is*

Susan Hawthorne is the author of seven collections of poetry. Her previous book, *Cow*, was shortlisted for the 2012 Kenneth Slessor Poetry Prize in the NSW Premier's Literary Awards, and was a finalist in the 2012 Audre Lorde Lesbian Poetry Prize (USA). *Earth's Breath* was shortlisted for the 2010 Judith Wright Poetry Prize. In 2013, Susan was the BR Whiting Library Resident in Rome funded by the Australia Council. She is a publisher and Adjunct Professor in the Writing Program at James Cook University in Queensland.

Other books by Susan Hawthorne

poetry

Valence: Considering War through Poetry and Theory (2011, chapbook)
Cow (2011)
Earth's Breath (2009)
Unsettling the Land (with Suzanne Bellamy, 2008, chapbook)
The Butterfly Effect (2005)
Bird (1999)
The Language in My Tongue (1993)

fiction

Limen (2013, verse novel)
The Falling Woman (1992/2004)

non-fiction

Bibliodiversity: A Manifesto for Independent Publishing (2014)
Wild Politics: Feminism, Globalisation and Bio/diversity (2002)
The Spinifex Quiz Book (1993)

anthologies

Horse Dreams: The Meaning of Horses in Women's Lives (with Jan Fook and
        Renate Klein, 2004)
Cat Tales: The Meaning of Cats in Women's Lives (with Jan Fook and Renate
        Klein, 2003)
September 11, 2001: Feminist Perspectives (with Bronwyn Winter, 2002)
Cyberfeminism: Connectivity, Critique and Creativity (with Renate Klein, 1999)
Car Maintenance, Explosives and Love and Other Contemporary Lesbian Writings
        (with Cathie Dunsford and Susan Sayer, 1997)
Australia for Women: Travel and Culture (with Renate Klein, 1994)
Angels of Power and Other Reproductive Creations (with Renate Klein, 1991)
The Exploding Frangipani (with Cathie Dunsford, 1990)
Moments of Desire (with Jenny Pausacker, 1989)
Difference: Writings by Women (1985)

LUPA AND LAMB

SUSAN HAWTHORNE

Published in Australia by Spinifex Press in 2014

Spinifex Press Pty Ltd
504 Queensberry St
North Melbourne, Victoria 3051
Australia
women@spinifexpress.com.au
www.spinifexpress.com.au

Cover design by Deb Snibson, MAPG
Back cover Medusa photo by Renate Klein, 2013
Text Box 1 2011, art and photo by Suzanne Bellamy, 2011
All other cover photos by Susan Hawthorne, 2013
Typeset by Claire Warren
Printed by McPherson's Printing Group

National Library of Australia
Cataloguing-in-Publication
Hawthorne, Susan, 1951–
Lupa and Lamb / Susan Hawthorne
9781742199245 (paperback)
9781742199214 (ebook : epub)
9781742199191 (ebook : pdf)
9781742199207 (ebook : kindle)
Includes bibliographical references
Poetry, Modern.
Imagist Poetry.
A821.3

Australian Government

Australia Council
for the Arts

This project has been assisted by the Australian Government through the Australia Council, its principal arts funding and advisory body.

PEFC
PEFC/21-31-16

There was a time when you were not a slave, remember that. You walked alone, full of laughter, you bathed bare-bellied. You say you have lost all recollection of it, remember ... You say there are no words to describe this time, you say it does not exist. But remember. Make an effort to remember. Or, failing that, invent.

— Monique Wittig, *The Guérillères*

per le mie innamorate, Renate e Freya

and for all the wolves, sheep and women
killed in the name of progress

contents

Main characters

Lupa/Ilia/Rhea Silvia/Acca Larentia/Diana/Artemis/Artemisia: these characters fold in and out of one another's stories. Lupa/Ilia/Rhea Silvia/Acca Larentia have the same identity; she is woman and a she-wolf. Linguistically, the word 'lupa' can mean both she-wolf and prostitute. Ilia/Rhea Silvia is raped by the god Mars and when she becomes pregnant, is imprisoned. Lupa, the she-wolf, finds Ilia's twins who are raised by Acca Larentia (also known as Lupa). Diana/Artemis/Artemisia is identified as a goddess, the mistress of the forests, of wolves; she who runs with hounds. As Artemisia she is a herb and the artist Artemisia Gentileschi, who was publicly scorned because she was raped.

Agnese/Santa Agnese/Saint Agnes was a Christian saint and martyr who was a virgin. She is often depicted holding or standing next to a lamb. The name Agnese comes from a Latinised form of the Greek word ‘αγνη (hagne), derived from ‘αγνος (hagnos) meaning chaste which, in turn, became associated with the Latin word for lamb (agnus). The lamb is an important early Christian symbol of innocence. Santa Agnese is the patron saint of rape victims and virgins. Her martyrdom occurred when she was just twelve or thirteen. On 21 January 304 AD, she was condemned to be dragged naked through the streets of Rome to a brothel. There, many attempts were made to rape her. Some of the men went blind. In one story she escapes by growing hair all over her body. Eventually she was beheaded.

Curatrix is the feminine of the word 'curator'; a guardian or custodian, she is also known as a healer, a woman who cures. Curatrix is the framer of this manuscript and responsible for collecting the 'lost texts'. The texts come from many different times, from the present to as far back as 300 000 years. Curatrix knows the voluminous variations of the histories of Rome and other places such as Sardinia, Malta, Etruria, Sicily. She is in charge of a new kind of museum, the Musæum Matricum (literally a place of the Muses/a musing place of the [f. pl.] Matrix/Mother/Source).

Sulpicia's dates cross the modern boundary between BCE and CE, although this boundary was not devised until 525 AD and not regularly used until the 800s. Sulpicia is the only woman whose poetry has survived in Latin from Ancient Rome. She lived during the reign of Augustus (63 BCE to 14 AD). Curatrix offers new interpretations of Sulpicia's work and together they unearth a new poem.

Livia (58 BCE to 29 AD), also known as Livia Drusilla, became Empress of Rome after her marriage (second) to Augustus. She was a powerful figure in Roman society, and mother and grandmother to later emperors. Livia was friends with Queen Salome of Judaea and, like Sulpicia, her life spanned the now BCE/CE boundary. Her house included a beautiful sunken room with garden frescoes. These can be seen in the Museo Massimo in Rome.

Preface by Curatrix

This manuscript has been drawn together in the lead-up to Livia's party. Women from many times and places were invited; some, like Diana and Agnese, arrived early and so, in good feminist spirit, I enlisted the assistance of my intern, Sulpicia, to help them find their way around Rome and nearby parts. As with all travel there were interruptions, missed buses, eye-opening places to see and histories to hear.

They visited the Musæum Matricum where I have gathered a series of lost texts from many periods. Some are recently found texts which have been published in obscure journals; others have never before been made public or have only been read by a few visitors to the Musæum.

The women visited Sardinia with its paleolithic, megalithic and Bronze Age treasures – of the last, the most spectacular being the nuraghe, stone towers built without mortar – and on Sardinia they also found those marvellous baetyls, small breasted stones. Indeed, a number of their travels involved breasted beings: birds, wolves, lions and more.

But then it was time to return to Rome and follow the stories of Lupa. These are retellings, some far more original than the ones we usually hear. Sulpicia became quite excited about the prospect of performing in a play and then reading aloud her own poems, which I have translated. And Psappha, too, joined us at the party to read her long forgotten poem.

Agnese said, it's all very well about these wolves and plays and poems, what about the lamb story? The lambs, it turns out, had a tough time of it, especially those who decided to take on the new faith, this 'Christianity'. They say it was quite different back then; women spoke sacred words and carried certain powers, especially the virgins. The stories are found in many languages, but we all have our mother tongue and we are more than capable of listening and learning.

In this manuscript I have translated as much as possible. And there is always the Internet or the Notes at the back of the book.

Before the party there was time to convene witnesses from a number of places: some long past; some contemporary. These re-memberings were important ways of bringing together new arrivals to the party. Some had travelled from the other side of the world and from the other side of time. Many had never before met.

And so we gathered, talked, shared stories, admired one another's hats, celebrated with food, drink, music and dance, argument and laughter and – as so often happens when feminists gather – a declaration was written up. This declaration represents our hope for the future.

Lupa

descent

the call
that hollow sound of Cumaea
I was here before
thousands of years ago

your hundred mouths
shouting
words frothed at the edge
of my mouth

the journey looming
flight into the unknown
descent into
the dark thighs of your cave

my hair snake-wreathed
Etruscan Medusa
speaking with a hundred voices
the sibilant hiss of prophecy

seizure grasped
I flail at vanishing memory
bruised rise from darkness
almost miss the plane

canis: Latin: dog

canis

my stars are in the constellation
of the dog
it's hot when Canicula rises
as hot as it gets

Canicula: Latin: little
dog, star constellation

at night we sleep in packs on rooftops
sharing grains herbs and wine
I've seen the wording
in the Etruscan museum
women depicted reclining
in ways that are suggestive of hedonism

how odd
when Socrates reclines with his pals
they call it philosophy
suggestive of intellectual activity

Artemis and Artemisia
I run with hounds
paint my revenge
in the eyes of Holofernes
I carry the stain

a bitter herb
I am of the forest
hunt when I must
but I prefer cushions
open fires roiling seas
nightwoods

and love

4

throw me to the wolves

love is sneaky creeps up from behind
surprises you at an intersection
shouts boo in the piazza

Venus sits with us over morning coffee
espresso doppio latte macchiato
and biscotti to share

are you your family's black sheep? I ask
my wolfish eyes on Agnese
wolf-bellied desire showing

as the moon sets we sit
on the roof terrace listening
bark of dogs distant howl of wolves

invitation

an invitation from Livia
to the party of the missing millennia
she's calling it the epochal reunion
good times for milliners

we have to wear a hat
be there on midsummer's day
Agnese I ask
have you seen her new extension?

sunken garden
dining room all in one
like the house of the Amazons
in Pompeii

with fruit trees
poppies oleanders
waterbirds and songbirds
makes you cool just to think of it

but we're too early
let's take one of those
open-air time tours
get on get off

we can satisfy
our appetites
our love
and this knee-capping lust

sheepish Agnese
stay in Roma
leave your fields
a few weeks

grass will grow
your flocks will thrive
I want to run wild
with you

turning point

aC BC
is it a band?

aC Avanti Cristo
who is he?

you'll find out soon enough
we could say BCE

AD anno domini
only one god?

how is it possible?
let's call it CE

the known world's
fulcrum

hop-on hop-off bus

from the temple of Venus where we make ancient vows
to the queen of heaven our witnesses wolfish and ovine
we head across the city but all the buses are stopped

marchers against the excesses of the curative industry
they have patented yet another formula of an old potion
claiming originality against the herbalists' memories

we pass Pantheon and parliament where a rock band sings against
millennia of corruption from the excesses of Caligula and Domitian
to Mussolini's megalomania and Berlusconi's bunga bunga dissipations

we press on to the wedding cake with its winged women and wolves
stopped by banners across streets buses emptied of passengers
at last we travel to Labia visiting Costanza at Agnese's insistence

Agnese is weaving through the ambulatory vault in a trance
as if following a sheep trail in these catacombs dedicated to her
where once sheep grazed and the mosaics still sing

Curatrix: tour of the lost texts

Musæum: Latin: place
of the Muses;
collection of rarities
Matricum: Latin (*f. gen.
pl.* matrix): of the
source; origin; mother

let me tell you something about myself
my job as curatrix of Musæum Matricum
is to excavate our history
to find the unfound and the unfindable

go in search of materials ignored
interpret those findings
sometimes with the help of a poet or artist
for academic tedium only gets you so far

the Cambridge school sniffs the wrong path
it cannot see what it is missing
I am going to show you things
those archaeologists deny

they should know since Marija and others
made it clear enough
but an intellectual non-sense
is like a minotaur in the labyrinth's heart

you'll get lost in the dark
and never find your way out
there are skeletons in this labyrinth
and for once they are not ours

Lost text: Ooss: dog three bones has
2011 CE

Rough translation

dog three bones has
moon time crunch time is
[what] is thrown is juggled; dogs howl [under the moon]
crescent moon centred fence [is]
fish swim [and?] encircle full moon
woman dilly bag carries
crunch time comes
she[?] the mountain path sees [follows] : moon sets

Transliteration

moon : crunch time : three bones : dog : has
fence : ( ) : ( ) : centred : crescent moon : howling dogs : throw : is juggled
woman : dilly bag : carries : full moon : fish : swim : encircle : ( )
moon sets : mountain : path : sees / follows : crunch time : comes

Notes by Curatrix

As is clear from this translation there remain many gaps in our understanding of Ooss. While somewhat ossified, the language does possess a certain transparency as well as some difficulties. The first thing to say is that the language, while partially pictographic, possesses indicators for complex tenses and verb structures. Like other ancient languages it has three persons: singular, dual, plural. One strange element is that only the feminine gender is found (with a few proto-archaic terms in neuter).

This poetic fragment is suggestive of a ritual in which the behaviour of dogs as the keepers of time is unsurprisingly given prominence. The only non-canine actor (the woman) is setting off on a pilgrimage of some sort (crunch time?).

The difficulty with the word 'reflected' is, I surmise, due to the lack of scent in a reflection, so the reflection's unreality is a conceptual lacuna. If the subject of the woman sentence had been a dog, the wide semantic arc would extend to the word 'smells', as well as 'sees' and 'follows'.

It is clear from the original sentence structure that what is before the snout is of prime importance. Furthermore, the moon, the dogs and the woman are in some kind of triangulated relationship with the fish, the sea and the reflected moon. Perhaps one trio indicates the mundane world, while the other has esoteric meanings. The question is, which is which?

what Lupa says

air is sweet in this forest as we follow
earth's ridge toward an Etruscan
hollow Diana running
alongside me

shrine of Demeter dug deep in soil
scraped from earth's heart
smells of two millennia
underworld protection

whiff of ancient rust of grain
her figure in an alcove wheat stalk
visible in her hand I sniff stale air
damp walls

nightfall we camp in ancient caves
Diana seeks traces
of handprints spirals whorls
rounded forms

in the space between night and day
air from Aurora's wings shivers
along my coat I curl into her belly
seeking warmth

rock temple holds us
through nocturnal hoots and howls
dawn birdcalls wake me
into saffron light

Diana laughs

wind lifts her hair
Curatrix has transported us to Sardegna
on the windy heights
rocks
rocks and more rocks

Diana absentmindedly picks artemisia
growing by the path
she's chewing on berries
and her dogs have sniffed out
the truffle patch

no words are needed
old stone women
atop the mountains
talk while sheep
graze the hillside

when we reach
the tempietto
silence drops over us
I touch my hand
heart to forehead

we visit the rock wombs
big enough to birth us both
fully grown
bones red painted
ready for the next life

Sardegna: Italian: Sardinia

tempietto: Sardinian: temple

wind howling
we are reborn
on the far side of the hill
on the outside an archaeological site
on the inside something more

nuraghe

Agnese and I wander
turn full circle
stare at the megalithic words

baetyl: Greek: baetylus
or baetulus: a sacred
stone or pillar

breasted baetyls and sickled menhirs
rocks piled in poetic structures

we walk hand in hand
between the lines
disappear behind towering boulders
put our ears to the rocks
listen to the songs

iynx: Greek: wryneck
(bird, woodpecker: *Jynx
torquilla*)

the breath of an iynx says Agnese
a wryneck flies between us
all a-hum
creation's breath
labyrinthine myths stories

we tread winding paths
a wall a dead end
spiralling through intangible space
retracing we find other pathways
different tales tucked into crevices

here a spinner
here a songster
stories buried by rockfall
by the passage of wind
and time

here walks the old one
a colossal stone
precariously balanced
like a spindle on her head
she walks and knits

purl one plain one
stories cleave in Sardinia
Scotland Malta
where giants built
mother-daughter temples

in Sardinia
words stream down
towering nuraghe
coalesce in swarms
of tears uncried

story stones

the god roared
throw away those story stones
they are no longer of any use

some died rather than throw away
the stories of the mothers and grandmothers
yarns dating to the beginning of time

some died in resistance to the god's orders
others caved in threw away the story stones
created great rubbles ruins of memory

when you've tossed them out
walk away do not look back
and so these lost ones walked

they walked away from their lands
away from their histories
away from their grandmothers' stones

ancient nerves

a day of ancient argument
when with zealous ear and helpless eye
I go in search of Etruscan relics
find italic grapes oozing sweet nectar
on a frieze birds tweeze worms from soil
ewe wolf uterine maze

night's death hour I wake
to a giant ginger object
rise and sink into oblivion
it was only the moon
sailing through cloud
breast parrot orange
on this feathered planet
or a brazen angel trumpeting dawn

Ilia's dream

circa 740 BCE

I know it is a dream but it doesn't help
every night I relive it
the old woman rushes in with her torch
river-wept in dream-shock
shouting my terrors

dear sister you are father-favoured
but he forsakes me in these hours
I tell you
life and energy abscond
abandon my whole body

the man who takes me
it is Mars
he is handsome and I am swept away
to an enchanted willow grove
embraced by the river

I am lost in that strange locale
my very self displaced
I am ravaged
and he laughs
sister afterwards I ache

I do not know up from down
earth sways at my every step
a disembodied voice sounds
our father Aeneas
you must bear these troubles alone

he does not comfort me
only the old woman with her trembling limbs
he does not come to me nor defend me
he kowtows to the one who calls himself god
as if this excuses rape

I reach my hands skyward
but all the words I hear are smooth-tongued
blandishments
I am heart-sick
and insomnia stalks my sleep

Lupa's story

circa 740 BCE

heat swells like distended breasts
the day after I whelp my cubs
my dugs full craving water
I wander the pink Palatino
to the cool by the river
flood-high from summer storms

zephyr: Greek: west
wind

I smell Zephyr's breath
hear the thin yelp
find them scratched and naked
tumbling from a wicker basket
I lick the caul from their bodies
first one then the other

they attach mouths to me
almost drain me of milk
like ringlets we curl in the grotto
I know the science of auspex
crows and ravens who bring
morsels of food augur well

there is man-smell in the air
I dare not remain
they are calm now
these pink-fleshed ones
I retreat from sun-glare
into the cave's umbral arms

22

ovine-faced Faustulus
steps from behind the fig tree
cradles them in sheepskin wrap
stares into my eyes bears them
to the breasts of lush Acca Larentia
who shares my name Lupa

Faustulus: Latin: from
the verb favere, to
favour; he is a
shepherd

Sabine women
720 BCE

history is being rewritten
it's not rape it's abduction
says Wikipedia that anonymous
unaccountable author

no sexual assault took place Livy says
can we believe him?

let's go over this as if in a court of law
it's a boy-gang led by Romulus
at a signal from him
all capture a woman from the rival gang

what do you think will happen
at this early stage?

let's now look at the Sabine men
they forbid their women to marry Romans
so the Romans conceive a big festival
invite the Sabines – especially the women

now what do you think?
was this a plan or something spontaneous?

the Romans under Romulus
have a deal up their sleeves
the women will have full property rights
and their children born free

does this suggest slavery
was the other half of the negotiation?

that's not a deal it's banditry
colonialism theft bondage
do the Sabine men give in first?
or the women because it is a lost cause?

no sexual assault took place Livy says
do you believe him?

crimes of men

in the imperial palace
Jupiter examines his conscience
finds it failing
but Romulus citizen son of Lupa
has no conscience to speak of
he tells us
don't worry you'll all be citizens with full rights
orders are orders they say
as they shame us
he thinks the sun rises from him
considers his power celestial
forgets that he started life
in a wicker basket on a river in flood
that he might have been food
that his life took a good turn
because of an alliance between
she-wolf and shepherd

diary of a vestal virgin

circa 15 BCE

it's hot the day they capture me
rake me from the line of candidates
along with my two friends
dutiful daughters of proud patriarchs
in the atrium vestae we are set to work
wool is our speciality
we scour comb and sing
we learn to spin and weave
follow the woof and warp
of the twisting threads

atrium vestae: Latin: house of the Vestal Virgins, Roman Forum

we learn the ancient poems
of Vesta hearth queen
foremother
we sing about
      Canuleia
      Veneneia
      Gegania
      Tarpeia
the prayers of power are long
we skip and run and chant
until they sing themselves

we tend Vesta's circadian fire
taking turns keeping it alight
with perilous punishments
for any girl who sleeps on the job

the river is our playground
we swim and collect water
from the nearby spring

we watch birds
learn the art of auspex

domus vestalis: Latin:
home of the Vestals

back in the domus vestalis
we prepare food for vesper rituals
and again for welcoming dawn
there's never any let up
always a sacred object to clean
or polish a vestment to weave
mola salsa to grind for Vestalia
a meal to make a song to learn
> Rhea Silvia
> Aquilia Severa
> Coelia Concordia
I like it here among the women

mola salsa: Latin: salted
flour

when I'm older I want to be
Virgo Vestalis Maxima
the holder of wills and testaments
I'll travel the forum in my cart
the new girls will braid my hair
> Aemilia
> Marcia
> Licinia
> Fonteia
> Fabia
> Rubria
I will heal with my hands and sacred words
even a look from me will save
no one will insult me for I am

sacrosanctitas: Latin:
inviolable

sacrosanctitas

Diana: drama queens

Sulpicia and Curatrix
want an extravaganza
the next text is a double act
I play Natī the wise
says Curatrix
Sulpicia makes a fine Śakuntalā
perhaps you would like to take the other roles
Diana and Agnese

a crowd appears from nowhere
they are scuttling about preparing the dais
on stage or off there's no distinction
we have scripts to read
there's not much here

I'll be Anasūyā says Agnese
I want to sing these lines

> *your lips are petals*
> *your arms are vines*

I am left to play Priyaṁvadā
never mind I muse
I get to adjust the garment
falling from Sulpicia's shoulder

sahīo: Prakrit: girl-friends, best friends (female), lovers

Natī: Sanskrit: actress

Vāc: Sanskrit: speech, goddess of speech

Prakṛtī: Sanskrit: nature, source, germ, seed, matrix

Śakuntalā: Sanskrit: Śakunta: bird; Śakuntalā was born in a forest and protected by birds.

Lost text: *Śaurasenī and Mahārāṣṭṛi Prakrits: Sahīo, a drama*

circa 1100–1200 CE

Natī: From water comes bubbling verse
she has many names among them
Vāc and Prakṛtī, source of seeds
source of words, the breeze that is speech.
Here comes the lovely Śakuntalā
and her two friends, sahīo who in sultry
weather weave petal-yellow earrings
while wild bees whisper secrets.

[*Three young women enter, walk around looking. Each is carrying a water jug appropriate to her strength.*]

Śakuntalā: Ido ido sahīo, come my sahīo.

Anasūyā: Sanskrit: without envy

Anasūyā: Halā, Śakuntalā. You spend so much time watering these plants anyone would think you were related.

Śakuntalā: We are, almost. This jasmine creeper is like my sister. Remember Urvaśī and how she became a jasmine vine pining for love? Who knows, this plant could be her arms. Its tendrils around the mango's trunk are fingers in the wind. The mango, its fruit is as sweet as any woman's body. Here [*mimes passing mango to Anasūyā*].

Priyaṁvadā: Sanskrit: sweet talker

Priyaṁvadā: See her suck the ripe fruit as if it were her lover's lips.

[*Anasūyā mimes wiping mango juice from her chin.*]

Offstage: Hey, wait a minute. What's all this Halā and words I can't
              understand. This play is meant to be in Sanskrit.

Natī: It's one of the Prakrits we women speak. It comes naturally to
              women. Woman to woman.

Priyaṁvadā: Śakuntalā, look at you. Come here a moment. Your bark
              garment is lopsided, falling off your shoulder.

Śakuntalā: Priyaṁvadā, you made it so tight I can hardly move. Anasūyā,
              come loosen this and sing for me.

Anasūyā: *your lips are petals*
              your arms are vines
              youth is rushing to make
              your limbs bloom
              let me draw these ties
              open so you can release
              your breath like
              a flower in spring

Natī: We are many-tongued. For prose we speak Śaurasenī. They say
              it was spoken at Mayura, but it's a matter of metaphor. We
              women like the colourful tail feathers, that's all. When we sing
              it's in Mahārāṣṭrī, beautiful and elegant words, a fan of
              peacock words.

[*The three young women laugh and dance. Their voices carry through leaves
like birdsong. Śakuntalā pauses at one of the trees, another jasmine creeper.
She runs her fingers along the climbing vine, pausing at each flower. She
presses her body to the tree, her nostrils fill with the scent of jasmine.*]

Anasūyā: Look out Śakuntalā, that bee is after you.

[*Śakuntalā steps back.*]

Śakuntalā:	I thought I heard a droning in my ears. Sahī, will it tell me something I want to hear?
Priyaṁvadā:	You know what they say about bees. A sign of love. Watch that the bee does not sting your lip, unless you want to be kissed.

madhukarī: Sanskrit: honey maker, bee

Anasūyā:	*oh madhukarī who hovers near* *whisper oh whisper in my ear* *dance bee dance me to the hive* *dance so that I too might fly*
Śakuntalā:	Oh Anasūyā, you are so full of songs. No bee is going to take to me. Only the moon is eaten away by love.

[*She begins a play of eyes. All three stand making eyes at one another in the ancient art of dṛṣṭi bheda.*]

Natī:	The goddesses of speech and knowing are numerous. There's Vāc and Prakṛtī herself, and no one can out-know Sarasvatī and her flowing underground words. Prakṛtī is elemental, the root form, the source, matrix and seed of the world.
Śakuntalā:	Anasūyā, sing me another old song.
Anasūyā:	*I don't know* *you at all* *but my heart* *is thundering* *in my chest* *my limbs* *a restless monsoon* *I am drenched*

Priyaṁvadā: What flavour, what rasa. I can almost taste your words, Anasūyā. Talking of taste, anyone hungry? Let's end our talk with food. How better to fill the senses and the belly.

[*The three young women pick up their water jugs, muttering soft words mixed with laughter as they disappear through the trees.*]

[END]

Notes by Curatrix

This little drama does not have a title, but sahī (*f. sing.*) is the Prakrit word for sakhī which refers to the friendship among the women in the play.

Natī in Sahīo opens with an eight-line poem honouring the goddesses of speech and language, the unknown author wishing for eloquence to be on her side. The opening utterances of Śakuntalā are 'Ido ido sahīo' and Anasūyā responds 'halā'. The first phrase means 'Come, girlfriends' while the second is a Prakrit word of greeting exchanged between the young women. They perform what is known in Sanskrit as a parikrama, a 'walking around' which announces the characters' intentions.

The figure of Śakuntalā is well known to Indian audiences and this playlet picks up on a number of these standard tropes. The mango is a metaphor for sulking love, jealousy, desire and a host of other feelings in Indian poetry.

It is difficult to call this a play, as it is not long enough. All the same there is some dramatic action occurring between Natī (perhaps a mentor) and these three teenage girls, who are too busy flirting with one another to notice much around them. It could be part of a longer play that has been lost. It was found among the belongings of an old woman, a Sanskritist. We don't know where she acquired this document. It is possible she made a trip to India in the 1970s at which time she would have been in her early fifties (she was ninety-five when she died). There was some puzzlement over the document and the rest might have been accidentally destroyed at that time. But this section appears complete, one scene depicting the story of Śakuntalā. It may have been written by an apprentice dramatist in the twelfth- or thirteenth-century court of King Lakṣmaṇasena of Bengal, when the Prakrits were a popular literary form.

salone

yesterday's performance was such fun
Agnese has found a new life
traipsing the boards singing her heart out
Curatrix has promised us something more
our very own poetry salon
with special guest our new friend
Sulpicia

in the twentieth century Joanna Russ
might have been writing about her

> She didn't write it.
> She wrote it but she shouldn't have.
> She wrote it but look what she wrote about.
> She wrote it but she isn't really an artist,
>   and it isn't really art.
> She wrote it but she had help.
> She wrote it but she's an anomaly.
> She wrote it BUT ...

enough of literary confection
on with the show

Curatrix introduces Sulpicia
some academics still doubt
her very existence

in 1978
Curatrix published an essay
challenging the view that
Uncle Tibullus wrote these poems
you listen and tell me later
if these sound like the work
of an old man

Sulpicia i

circa 12 BCE

finally a love that knocks me sideways
how can I hide it?
this is no shame

my muse in love
and love itself release me
from all my promises

amorous Venus sent her
we lie breast to breast
aching with desire

dare I make my love public
with this poem?
why not?

Sulpicia ii

circa 12 BCE

hateful birthday is upon me and I'm meant to go to that irksome country farm
you expect me to leave Ms Deliziosa who gets to stay in the city
sweet Roma where else would you want to be?
what's a girl to do in a country villa
where that frigid river runs through Arretium's land?
Auntie I know you want what's best but your fierce protectiveness is too much
I'm in no mood for travel my heart isn't in it
         – and you always win

Sulpicia iii
circa 12 BCE

you know I'm in seventh heaven sad no longer
I get to stay in Roma for my birthday
all our days – even my birthday – are driven
by that chance of lady luck we were hoping for

Sulpicia iv
circa 10 BCE

be thankful I'm not as carefree as you
now that you are truly tactless
will you be at pains to pass up on any stola
or pretty young thing with a wool basket under her arm?
        is she as good as Sulpicia?
my friends worry I'm getting into bed with a worthless unknown

Sulpicia v
circa 10 BCE

do you care at all that your lover – me –
is worn out by tossing and turning with fever?
this body will not overcome its depressing ills
nor I suppose will it improve unless you –

        but what's the point of recovering
        if your heart is so apathetic

Sulpicia vi

circa 10 BCE

I wish your passion for me would burn out
as it did for me the day before yesterday
if I've ever done anything so senseless
which now I regret all the more
it was leaving you alone last night
wanting to conceal my burning lust

Sulpicia's lost poem

Sulpicia breaks her recitation
the next poem remained hidden
she says
until one day
I was clearing out some old papers
there it was in the corner of the vault
covered in dust
forgotten

Lost text: Latin: Sulpicia vii

circa 6 or 7 CE

I was so young with fire in my heart
and I didn't know how to measure
the feelings that flared
was it the right time to let go
to leave
          – or not?
but damn it
you could have convinced me to stay
dear one
why didn't you try?

Notes by Curatrix

Regrets in love … a young person's problem. And Sulpicia's opportunities
were nothing compared to that flirt Catullus: neither in love, nor in poetry.
She told me she'd been head-over-heels in love with her, Ms Deliziosa, but
only later did she wonder what might have happened had she stayed. Would
they have gone down in history as the famous Latin Sapphics? But I say, give
up the regrets and live for now. It is not long before party time.

Pompeii
79 CE

Curatrix says
let me divert you for a day
her tour not the adolescent thrill
of a romp with members

lupanaria: Latin:
brothels

latrines and lupanaria
she sweeps up the Vesuvial detritus
reduces the myth of debauchery
to a single brothel

takes us on rambles through temples
unravelling their secrets
on the way out
cave canem beware the dog

cave canem: Latin:
beware the dog

says the sign at the portal in Pompeii
filled out in coloured mosaic
there is no poet
no tragic performance

depicted there
the reading of an oracle
the one that says Alcestis
must die in the first pages of the play

she hears the oars of the ferryman
servant of Thanatos
she dies for husband Admetus
the queen who dies is not revered

Sulpicia's grammar lesson

the library has outgrown its space
and I am caught on the bluff of books
needing a harness to rappel this precipice

as if it's not enough to die for another
at the base of the cliff is plastered
a sheet bearing this quote

> If x was the sound representing the idea of a wolf,
> y a lamb, and z the act of killing,
> then xyz or xzy could be a comprehensible sentence,
> representing the idea of a wolf killing a lamb.

but I'm a vegetarian and have no wish
to kill a lamb for dinner
or for poetry

xyz says Diana

I am x and you are y
we should be enemies
but we are lovers
Agnese and I

let's get some history straight
I came to you
that winter when it was so cold
you already had lambskin
wrapped around your body
so let's not deflect responsibility

if x was the sound
representing the idea of wolf
y a lamb and
z the act of loving
xyz

Agnese says
I am y and you are x
I should fear you but I don't
there are more of us
we vibrate when our noses
catch scent

I am trying says Diana
to refuse meat
just because I like it
doesn't mean I should indulge

it's not okay answers Agnese
pain does not make me kind
recovery is millennia long
the scars are visible still
but I am resilient
my story can wait

Lost text: Aeolic Lesbian: Psappha in slippers
circa 565 BCE

you young ones bound to the Muses' sweet-smelling gifts
you are fervent songsters your voices clear as the lyre

once my body was soft tender to touch but old age
has taken its pleasure turning my black hair white

my heart is heavy my knees in youth as light-
footed as the dancing deer no longer carry me

now I sigh in surprise but what am I to do?
aging is human there is no way out

even Tithonos who was borne to the far ends
of the earth by lovesick Dawn

young and enchanting at first was haunted
by grumbling old age despite his immortal wife

Notes by Curatrix

For years they have been saying there are no more poems by Psappha to be
found, that we must content ourselves with fragments. This poem gives me
hope. I am sure that hidden among the dusty papyri we will find yet more
poems by the tenth muse.

When we think of Psappha, or Sappho as she is more commonly known, we
tend to think of a youngish woman not more than about forty years of age.
But Psappha lived to be somewhere between sixty and seventy-eight years
old. In her histories we hear fabrications such as her suicide for the love of
Phaon. For a poet to have a reputation such as hers, to be the 'tenth muse' as
Plato called her, she must have lived long enough for news of her poetry to
travel as far as it did.

In the text, Psappha accepts that aging is part of being human. Like Ovid, in Elegy XIII of his *Amores*, she compares the human experience to that of the gods. Poor Eos, goddess of dawn, is lumbered with an aging Tithonos, because wishing for eternal life is no good unless it comes with eternal youth.

Diana shears Livia's flock

shearing days are here
the flock is bleating
something is unsettling them
they run in circles
making trouble for me

driving the flock is a dog
or is it a wolf?
entre chien et loup
at dawn it's hard to tell
is it work or food?

entre chien et loup:
French (lit): between
dog and wolf

the shears are sharp
my arms strong
one at a time
it's a trust thing
she has to relax

fold her into your knees
with a firm but not tight grip
hold her close
begin on the soft belly
and back leg

dance your way
and step through
to neck and shoulders
so intimate a move
her head tipped sideways

not done yet
here come the long strokes
hip to head
on the home turn
clip the last fleece

spread it
like the coverlet of a bed
curled and cosy
the thread strong
next winter's warmth

anoint each sheep
with a concoction
prepared ahead of time
in three days
wash and dress her

Agnese spins Livia's clip

tease and comb
sing the wool
vibrate the thread with bow
a method from the old ones

spinsters are at wheels
yarn between fingers and lips
in the atrium of Livia's house
where all can see her productivity

weavers patterns looms
their clackety-clack
against the whirr of the wheels
craftswomen counting threads

I make the best garments in Rome
light as Arachne they float in summer air
in winter warm as–   as lambswool
we call the first comb virgin

Lamb

Curatrix to Agnese

Agnese a treat for you
I hear you have a passion for sheep
you keep them close

I have seen the statue
in la Basilica di Santa Cecilia
she with her harp

you with a lamb
tucked under your arm
our next lost text is about sheep

so underrated
my darling ones
says Agnese cheesily

Lost text: Vedic: edī and avidugdha

circa 1100 BCE

edī

bright light in the east
unravelling darkness
a path for the sun between clouds

avidugdha

blue sheep
white sheep
make curd for the gods

avidugdha

churn amṛta
raise urns of milk
spill it on earth

edī

your fleeces shining
wishing not for fame but love

if only the devī will give it

Notes by Curatrix

The Vedas are singularly lacking in poems about sheep. An unusual circumstance since, prior to the sixth millennium BCE, Proto-Indo-European (PIE) peoples raised sheep. It looks as though at some unknown time the sheep was trumped by the larger animals – horses and cows. The sheep continued to be revered in out-of-the-way places at the edges of what is called 'civilisation'.

Generally, these people passed their songs and poems down orally and only rarely committed them to writing. This fragment was found on a clay urn, which perhaps had been used for holding milk. Unfortunately, the urn was shattered and so we have only this translation made by an over-excited on-site poet to go on.

We are lucky to have found this short and rather enigmatic poem about sheep. Edī is Sanskrit for 'ewe' and avidugdha indicates a milk-producing sheep (avi: sheep + dugdha: milked, suckled, related to the English word 'dugs'). The poem, which was probably sung, comes from a valley where men are reputedly not permitted permanent residence (though they must have at some time in the distant past, since this poem is in Vedic). The women swear by this history and state that it has always been thus. They make the most beautiful cloths, fine-spun and warm. When pressed about men, they laugh and say, of course we know how to keep the generations going; we are sheep herders after all, but that does not mean we should share our quarters with men. Do as sheep do, they chuckle, flock together. Those rams can find their own way.

Of the sheep, they say, they give us milk and strong cheeses, their wool keeps us warm in winter and their droppings provide us with information about the future. They add that the sheep is the foremost constellation of the year. They call her the energiser, the front-runner; they admire her tenacity.

The women tell us this is a very old song. It contains a reference to the story about the origins of the world through the churning of milk. The milk is usually (and they say mistakenly) referred to as cows' milk. The women say that the cow is a later variation on the story. They add that there are tales of fleeces with words inscribed on the leather pelt. None can verify this, but we should not dismiss it out of hand. Stranger methods of inscription have been known.

Basilica Santa Maria degli Angeli e dei Martiri

angel: from Greek:
ángelos (αγγελος):
messenger

martyr: Old English
martir, via ecclesiastical
Latin from Greek
martur: witness

the angels are gathering
for Livia's party
in this place of memory
for virgin martyrs

they are stars
they constellate
across the centre of this church
earth's ecliptic
planetary pearls
laid out like an Italian feast
here are the sheep
cows and devilish twins

the old ones are here too
come to see the layout
the spread
across the transept
la linea meridiana

la linea meridiana:
Italian: a line struck by
the sun at midday

just as our ancestors did
here light falls
indicating the equinox
the lamb tells us
with precision
when spring has come

the world according to Santa Barbara

La Barbe
a group after my own heart
these women wear fake beards
speak their minds in men's halls of power
they say in no uncertain words
avete rotto enough is enough

La Barbe: French: the
bearded one; colloq:
enough is enough; a
French feminist protest
group [see notes]

avete rotto: Italian:
enough is enough

I storm men's bastions
I did in my first life and I'll keep doing it
I have my reasons

first they called me barbarian
baa-baa they tormented and teased
because I didn't speak their language
I'm an outsider
always will be

barbarian: Greek:
barbaros (βαρβαροσ):
barbarian

barbarian sticks they call me Barbara
my family are traders
Father has big plans for me
thinks he'd like me to marry up
perhaps a courtier
so to keep me 'in tact'
he shuts me in a tower with just two windows

word has been going around
a new cause
sounds good
peace and innocence
resisters of empire
soft as lambs
like I said we are traders

and before my father heads off on a long journey
he orders a bathhouse built for me

San Giovanni Battista:
Italian: Saint John the
Baptist

I saw San Giovanni Battista
standing waist-deep in water
he poured water all over me

I resume my room
open a third window
in the tower
when my father returns he is aflame with rage
he is not a man of the trinity
my conversion worse for him
than the loss of my virginity

he denounced me
my own father

they came with burning torches
the fires went out

they tried to scorch my skin
but it blew back at them

despite the inferno
my wounds healed overnight

anger flared in their eyes
brighter than the burns on my breasts

it is my father
sent to separate my head from my body
his final betrayal

on the way home
I incinerate that father of mine
send a bolt of lightning
with every pore of hatred in my body
every wound they made
now he is gone

but my lives continue
those bastions of male powder kegs
miners artillery men bomb disposers
they love me more than anyone
the numbers men too
countless mathematicians

Santa Barbara (Italian),
Sainte-Barbe (French,
obsolete), and
santabárbara (Spanish):
powder magazine, the
most explosive place in
ships and fortresses

gun powder fires their imaginations
with their flares and smoke
these boys love the loud bangs
they name them after me

come to kill us

the wolves have come to kill us
slavering for our deaths
in pursuit their red tongues hang out

child Cecilia
they forced you to marry
but you were smart
and convinced Valerianus to join you
in non-consummation
when did wilful virginity become a crime?

the steambath torture failed
a beheading was ordered
three times they tried and failed
your death as drawn out
as a funeral dirge
like Orpheus
your bodiless head crooned
sang alleluias to the glory of God

the wolves have come to kill us
slavering for our deaths
in pursuit their red tongues hang out

lambkin Agnese
pure as virgin wool
your good name and family
could not save you from the wolf
lupanar: Latin: brothel   they lured you to the lupanar
you would be no lupa
though hair grew on your body
pimps and rapists were struck blind

58

even the fire they lit would not burn
and so they beheaded you

we have not forgotten you
Papa wears the pallium
lambs come in wicker-baskets
with blue ribbons to Santa Cecilia
on the feast day of Santa Agnese
we tend these lambs
shear spin and weave the pallia
for he who leads the flock
we sing the Agnus Dei
dona nobis pacem

the wolves have come to kill us
slavering for our deaths
in pursuit their red tongues hang out

pallium: Latin: mantle,
coverlet

Agnus Dei: Latin: Lamb
of God, referring to
Jesus

dona nobis pacem:
Latin: grant us peace,
from the Agnus Dei of
the Roman Catholic
Mass

black sheep

sono una pecora nera
a throwback a crossbred
some say I'm peccatrix
a woman full of peccato
peccato originale
I'd rather peccato veniale
or un peccato di gioventù
the indiscretions of the young
who should be put out to pasture
and not talked to until next pasqua
when they will shear my virgin wool

a pascolare o non
to graze or not to graze
tutti pregano per me
they take up a precative stance
pray to you la pecora
when we gather together in Latin
they call our collective pecus
we pasture in the pascuum
the battle between Latin and Italian
fought out over the bodies of lambs
the minds of wolves

I have a secret to tell
it wasn't the wolf in lamb's clothing
we sheep tricked the wolf
in the guise of innocence
we stole everything that was hers
with some good marketing
gold and other precious metals
we swung the pendulum our way

who believes in the innocence of wolves
who says that lupa cannot be deceived
as they say in the mass
preghiamo
perdona i nostri peccati

preghiamo: Italian: let us pray

perdona i nostri peccati: Italian: forgive us our sins

Lost text: Kartvelian: Medea's lambs
1200 BCE

the day the Cyclops lamb
was born the people began to talk

she tends it like a child
we've seen her feed it
milk squeezed from a bag
shaped like an old ewe's udder

we've seen her push her own
nipple into the mouth of this
one-eyed monster it gazes
love-sick its one eye growing
full as the moon

but what can we do?
it's her flock she is their mother
and like any mother she picks
the strangest among them
to carry out her tasks

remember the breach-birth
black lamb seven summers ago
how she pulled it from the ewe's
womb breathed life into it
then fed herbs to the poor
exhausted mother

the black lamb of the white
mother coming feet first into
the world – everything backwards
everything topsy-turvy what
omens does she crave?

yet they thrive – these strange
and backward ones – she has
a way with herbs and magic
and though we speak about it
in whispers among ourselves we
dare not speak in the marketplace

where unknown ears may hear
and carry away our words

Notes by Curatrix

The name Medea is not mentioned directly in this poem but contextual
evidence suggests that it is indeed about Medea. It is likely one of the lost
texts from the fragmentary epic, the *Little Iliad*. This work describes the shift
from chthonic deities to sun worship and an all-powerful male god or trinity
of gods.

Medea is readily identified here by the reference to Circe who is her aunt
(sister of Aeëtes, 'keeper of the Golden Fleece', Medea's father and King of
Colchis), and by the references to her use of herbs and healing. The story of
the Cyclops lamb is an odd one, as it suggests later stories about Cyclops in
The Odyssey might have their origins in this tale.

The speaker of this poem reveals distress at the way in which the world is
changing. The poem, though likely dated around the time of the Trojan War
(circa 1200 BCE), could be as late as 700 BCE.

Sant' Angela di Merici on the precative

precative: from Latin
precatus, past
participle of precari:
entreat, pray

the precative is a mood she inhabits
she is inclined that way
she prays
she beseeches an invisible being in precatory ways

Priscilla says it's sensible
that she be in a precative mood
the word itself asks to be revealed
an old root

√prcch: Sanskrit:
beseech, pray

√prcch
the verb to ask
related to precarious
it's risky to pose too many questions

Joan and the Johns

the Johns are a confusing lot
there are Johns and Joan
antipopes
un-number Johns

the trouble starts
with tenth century
John XIV
a mere nine months before
prison and death

in 1099 Joan
(or maybe the 850s)
Johannes Anglicus
(for she is German
of English parentage)
but talk of her now
she is La Papessa Giovanna

smart as periwinkle
she outdoes them all
in language arts and scripture
until that day of parturition
all too public
between the dentures of
the Colosseum
and the dendrites of
San Clemente

a street shunned
for centuries
with blood on its
cobbles
birth blood
blood of death

between John XIVb
and John XXIII
come antipopes
a muddle of popes
popes with multiple
numberings
un-numbering the orders
but none more so
than Joan

the calculus of umbrals

the sheep bleat
in the calculus of umbrals
the shadowy variable
allows pretence to become proof

San Clemente
has thirteen sheep
above this coven of sheep
the tree of life multiplies
calculates infinity
becomes the world tree
its branches spiralling endlessly
the sheep are breeding
producing new flocks
same same each year
and the shepherds endlessly at work

in the calculus of umbrals
the shadowy variable
allows pretence to become proof

but says the man of God
this *eternal circling* is *futile*
it is *endless repetition*
what we need is progress

the shadowy variable
allows pretence to become proof

that *vain circular motion*
is broken open by the cross
the new dynamic of a world
no longer circling but ascending

allows pretence to become proof

the *fishhook of God*
has put human history
on the up and up
we men are your branches
death is love
we have taken over
we are ascending
to the fathers' *true progress*

the shadowy variable
allows pretence to become proof

earth shatters
branches break
the cycle is broken
broken open
the forest shattered
broken open
clear felled

in the calculus of umbrals
the shadowy variable
allows pretence to become proof

the cross hewn
the man crucified
broken open
the cross has changed the dynamic
now human history is on the up and up

the sheep bleat
in the calculus of umbrals
the shadowy variable
allows pretence to become proof

Notes by Curatrix

I really should not interfere here, because this is not a Lost Text, but I just have to say that the power of mathematics depends on the use to which it is put. Santa Barbara has her followers (and it is all very well to know how to use explosives), but we have to remember that 'mathematics' is from the Greek word mathanein (μαθάνειν), 'to learn'. Mathematics can be sublime, just as poetry can be. Poetry admits that it is an inexact science, that it is based on associative thinking; and the best mathematicians I know also do this. Then they run the exacting proof.

Calculus is that 'as if' moment. Symbols take the reader into strange new places. Or as Virginia Woolf says in her essay 'A Sketch of the Past', "we are the words; we are the music; we are the thing itself." By 'pretence' above, I do not mean 'misleading' but 'wonderful'; wonderful in the way that Woolf's perceptions give that sense of 'wonder'.

Lost text: Etruscan: ativu and atinacna

circa 1500 BCE

ativu: Etruscan: mother
atinacna: Etruscan:
grandmother

ativu [and] atinacna
[and] maternal relatives
[   ] made an offering
ritual vases [   ] circle
each [   ] proper measure

I felt the wind shift
as if someone gusted past

consecrated oil
honeyed wine
poured in honour
[   ] a libation

atinacna
haruspex
removed her ritual mask
calling the ancestors to heel
she draws signs
from entrails

[   ] night came
sky smiths
stoked the stars
they shone more brightly than usual [before now]

the home sheep so quiet
waiting for something
a flurry
a breath of grass

half-moon cake rose
we sang
in time with the owl
uh-huh uh-huh

a whole night we sang
waiting for the spirit's flight
by dawn lupu was gone

lupu: Etruscan: the
body lying flat

moon vanished in sun and cloudmist
we stopped singing
took up our flutes and whistles
chased the spirit
called out
quick follow that moon

afterwards I saw my mother
braid her hair
[   ] her sister
scratched words into the clay vase
[   ] the centre of the circle
carried it
      [   ] stone house

[   ] late afternoon
we sat again
breast to breast

[text breaks off here]

Notes by Curatrix

This poem has been re-membered from fragments found in an Etruscan
necropolis. While it has been possible – after several years of painstaking

work – to put the words together (a poet was needed to help in this task), we believe we now have a text as close to the original as possible.

The title of the poem is a reference to the mother [ativu] and the grandmother [atinacna]. These two words are terms of endearment, so it becomes immediately clear that the author/speaker is the child of this mother. As only the maternal relatives appear to be present, we can readily say that the child is a daughter. This is borne out by the term 'breast to breast' in the final stanza we have available.

The poem describes a night ritual that takes place following the death of the speaker's aunt [mother's sister, sometimes called moster]. The grandmother is regarded as having powers of future sight. An haruspex is a person who can read the entrails of animals.

The wind appears to be an important player in the dispersal of the mother's sister's spirit: not only the wind itself, but the uh-huh singing followed by the playing of wind instruments at dawn.

The word 'lupu' has not been translated because there is no easy way to do so in English. Lupu refers to the body, lying flat. It signifies that the spirit, the person who formerly held that body, has now released her grasp and has left the house of the body. The wind instruments are picked up as both a farewell and a reminder to any dawdling spirit that now it is time to leave.

Angelic: ancestors of Curatrix

they are birds
my ancestors

we were the first
we winged ones
are souls
we free the dead
release their spirits

all the old ones have wings
and when they came
        to change the world into carrion
they tied him to a cross
wings outspread

the old ones weren't fooled
but the young striplings
made of him a god

that's why I'm here
to forge memories
        avian
        angelic
        harpic

Echidna will breed more monsters
Hydra will speak from her hundred mouths
Cerberus will cease howling
the Gorgon's hair will writhe
Medusa will laugh again

bring me feathers
bring me wingbones
I'm ready for the rising thermal

my ancestors
they are birds

Domitilla and Priscilla

the bus takes us
to the galleria femminile
Agnese's ancestors

honey-combed earth
each cavity a resting place
wrapped in cloth

after a year we bring gifts
come with oil lamps
break bread

in the tiny alcove
we sing their spirits
to eternal heaven

how she stands
arms reaching skyward
rejoicing in speech

god is a bird
alighting on the head
floating away

for Santa Cecilia

under the apse
a pure white marble body
hands bound head wrapped
face downward crying

she sings through her dead mouth
the earth hears her long dying song
above golden angels spiral
and my heart weeps

crimes of women

each day there is more bad news
today it is Anastasia
they say she walks like a man
abandon her
they say she has died in her cave
alone

last week it was Susanna and Balbina
marriage resisters
they refuse the hands of men
it does them no good
even though Susanna makes miracles
healing the infirm

they've taken Lucia to the lupanar
the same brothel
where they killed Agnese
I am impenetrable
Lucia is unmovable untouchable
a paragon

Sicilia: Santa Felicita

in a glass case
the body of Santa Felicita
beneath the crucified Christ
and the relics of twenty-eight martyrs
who died in imitation

Carthage, Tunisia: Santa Perpetua
6 March 203

last night I climbed a bronze ladder
with weapons hanging from it
but the dragon was too far away
and I could not reach it

my father wants me to recant
but I cannot this faith is too precious
and my dear companion Felicity
stays with me giving strength

in my dream the dragon
does not bring harm I climb
and climb the walls into Paradise
suffering is my lot

Lost text: Akkadian: if I were booty

circa 1790–1745 BCE

they don't like me
nor the cuneiform words
I have carved [   ] tablets
late night
[   ] last new moon
under the chisel of darkness
they came [   ] me

first they smashed my words
ground the shards
bevelled my arguments
bound [   ]
as for a shroud
with spiral binds
they came [   ] me

walls sink into night
stone-thick and silent
the floor is rock-rough
[   ] rebel but no soldier
and if I were booty
I'd be treated better

they will come [   ] me
and when they do
I'll say remember the warriors
treat me as you do them

Eristi-Aye (c.1790–1745 BCE) was an Akkadian writer. This poem was unearthed from a deep stone room, protected over many years. Prior to its discovery we had only a quotation from the poem, which read: 'But remember this: / even warriors seized as booty in war / are treated humanely. / At least treat me like them.'

This discovery, which was carved into stone, appears to be the original poem composed while Eristi-Aye was behind high walls. To be a woman is crime enough and she must have been imprisoned for an extended period of time in order to have carved out this poem. Eristi-Aye is one of the earliest known incarcerated writers. Several decades ago, scholars discovered further lines suggesting her imprisonment was organised by her parents using falsified tablets, what we today refer to as fabricated evidence.

Australia and Italy: lupa girls

we are lined up like soldiers at a draft
they pull us out one by one
record our names unusual attributes
fat big tits large bum weird look in eyes
that sort of thing

they are not interested in us
just how we measure up
to some unstated norm
we know it isn't fair
but it doesn't stop us from competing

the redhead is pulled out first
they write 'big tits' next to her name
give her eleven out of ten
she is loud full of bravado
doesn't hurt me she brags

when it's my turn
I am scared
my legs like jelly I try not to tremble
I piss myself (just a little)
it makes me stand up straight

for the rest I hardly remember
I am in an old building
a church but not like ours
they come in one after another
grab at me tear my clothes

my breasts are bared
it is cold they punch me
knock me to the floor
tear my skirt
I leave the scene of the crime

the pain is unendurable
shoots through me like an iron rod
at the forge my skin burns
flares red I hear one cry out
she's possessed as the gods seize me

Palermo, Sicilia: inquisition

death rides a skeletal horse
corpses trampled
a woman's silent scream
arrow in her throat

inmates draw
the moon dog devil
the faithful kneel
naked in penitence

whispers of sin
hell of sleep
endless pain
help us oh lord

someone here knows
the Nicean creed
writes on the wall
with anxious hope

    tortura
    brutalità
    atrocità

Tuscany: Il Giardino dei Tarocchi

Il Giardino dei Tarocchi:
The Tarot Garden

she lives inside the sphinx
a mirrored cavern
bent with broken glass

the right nipple
a window on the world
breakfast eaten by the left

the devil is not her
he is her past
father vile daddy

she builds giant tarocchi
like memories of nuraghi
intangible space

powerful she figures
the empress a house
death a new beginning

Australia: sheep town
1961 CE

sheep town scandal
five hundred residents
hushed but even
school children hear

sons of well-to-do farmers
on charges of rape
whispers on the phone
sudden silences

I scour
the newspapers
for that year
there is no record

Lesbos: aidos

aidos: Greek: shame

I want to tell you what happened
but how to put it into words
how can I say the words
when my body is the crime

Cavalupo: Latin: quarry
of the wolf

Etruria: Cavalupo

in the quarry of the wolf
the remains of two women
they have shared this urn
for three thousand years

your body on my tongue
your tongue on my body

once we were birds
winged auguries
between us multiple breasts
wolf paws and tail

your blood on my tongue
your tongue on my blood

two women lope in parallel
noses twitching airborne scents
thigh muscles rippling
pounce and prance the wolf dance

Lost text: Linear A: twenty-seven wethers

circa 3900 BP

Rough translation

she carries a small gilded tripod
from Messara comes golden wheat
cooked in saffron
the shepherdesses bring the wethers from the hills
twenty-seven
fresh figs and dried figs are piled high
golden wine spills from conical cups
the people feast under the full moon

Transliteration

vessel : three legs : diminutive ending : of gold : carries [f.]: she [honorary voc.]
direction : place name? : movement towards : grain : of gold
[verb] : spice / herb /plant [crocus?] : of gold
shepherds [f.] : sheep : 27 : high
figs : green : figs : black : high
conical cups : liquid : of gold : high
people : food : moon

Semantics

small bronze tripod gilded she carries
from place name Messara [near Phaestos] to this place
golden grain [wheat]
[transformation verb?] : spices of golden thread [saffron]
shepherds [f.] sheep [n. – wethers] : 27 : high [from]
green figs [fresh figs] black figs [dried figs] : high
conical cups : golden liquid [wine] : high
people food [feast] : round moon

Notes by Curatrix

The interesting thing about this short text is the interweaving images and metaphors. The colour gold is a trope that saturates the text. Height is also important: in one instance it means 'from the heights', in others it suggests 'cornucopia'. A feast or festival is taking place and a woman is carrying a small vessel that can stand on its three legs (perhaps a reference to Trivia). Young women bring in the sheep which have been neutered. Oddly the number twenty-seven is specified. It is unclear what significance this number has, although it is possible that the magical nature of 3x3x3 (3 cubed) might be referenced; it is also unclear whether or not the sheep are to be killed (ritually) or eaten as part of the feast, or whether these people eat mainly grain, herbs and fruits. If the sheep were to be ritually slaughtered one would expect some sense of the sacrificial to be evident in the poem.

All the actors in this short text are female, from the unidentified 'she' at the beginning of the poem, to the shepherdesses. The sheep would once have been male, but have been castrated; the neuter gender is therefore employed – they are wethers, not rams. While this is a short fragment, the fragment itself is complete. As for the unnamed 'she' in the poem, we know she is a woman with ritual power, through the use of an honorary vocative case. The age of the shepherdesses is indicated by a word which suggests they have not yet reached puberty.

It is possible the text refers to a puberty rite in which only women participate, as Spyridon Marinatos (1976) notes. Nanno Marinatos (1984) suggests saffron was used in rites of passage for young women because of its effectiveness against menstrual cramps. The full moon is also suggestive of a puberty rite.

Delos: homeless Latona

my mother's needs were terrestrial
she had no place on earth
to give birth to me and my brother
it was Hera who banned her
shunned by the people
she would not give birth on terra firma
neither any island
nor stable nor inn
nor any place under the sun

she had walked twelve days
twelve months twelve years
an eon heavy with gravity

from the icy land of Hyperborians
to the floating island of Delos
barren as Nauru
no umbilicus attached to earth
I came first
(some say on the quail island of Ortygia)
and bright spark that I am
I became her midwife
in the birthing of my twin

Hyperborians: from
Greek: people from
beyond the north wind

daughter of Sun and Moon
she was the turning point
the spindle of destiny
spun between the ages
the old world and the new
where lupa gave way to lupo
some say her name means forgetful
from lethe or lotus
fruit of oblivion

but Latona is the year's round
the twelve month dance
of sun and moon

Australia: memory's labyrinth

my grandmother's needs were architectural
they arched stretched out over lawns
rose like great temple ceilings
they never lounged about ate chocolate
or wasted time in street-corner conversation
she was like a homestead with a return verandah
that looked out over paddocks
took in the whole landscape
and everyone who wandered or sped by

my grandmother was called ferocious
she took the world in her stride
insisted on respect and courtesy
gave a dressing down to the uncouth
on picnic race days she made sandwiches
not wanting to waste hours on competitive cooking
her bets were selected with determination
and she won more often than not
once she won at eighty to one
the bookie almost bankrupt

my grandmother perished as she had lived
the family waited for resurrection
not believing such a force of nature
could go so fast leaving nothing but dust
for the most part my grandmother is forgotten
except by the girl she told stories to
great architectural tales that wound through forests
took labyrinthine detours but always returned
to the space between them and silence

hypogeum, also
hypogaeum (pl.
hypogea): Greek: hypo:
under; gaia: earth,
earth goddess

Malta: hypogeum

we came in small boats
with sows goats sheep
for we are farmers
our knowledge is of animals
and seasons

we watch the cycles
summer to winter
watch the growth
spring to autumn
life to death

when our animals die
their bones are left
in open air it brings
more scavengers
more birds

when we die
vultures tear tissue from bone
but the spirit remains
until it is returned
to the womb of the earth

seven thousand years
my spirit still dwells here
with seven thousand souls
a temple carved in soil
helical ceiling of stone

on the walls ochre spirals
statuettes among the skeletons
my figure lying
head upon hand
body at rest

they visit and sing the songs
taught them so long ago
they bring gifts of limestone and clay
if only they knew how small we are
our bones only half the story

Ġgantija, Malta: archaeology

we build tenements of giants
our temples magnificent
you declare our calendars crude
doubt that we made the plans
based on our own female form

you who don't see
mother-daughter temples
deny us like so many generations
you compare our bodies
to Sumo wrestlers

dwell on the hips
flesh of the belly
beauty of those breasts
shoulder blades
could be wings

Malta: Curatrix

not a whisper on this headland
over the islet of Filfla
wind still stand still

    a museum cluttered with static
    the poster depicts a wrestler
    his body the wrong shape
    hips too narrow shoulders too broad

ancients try to speak
but not a word is heard
her mouth breathless

    in the hollows of the rock
    a round space empty
    cut right through the sarsen
    a female space

old ones sing the silence
Mnajdra's walls her stone slabs
absorb sea wave sound wave

    back in the Musæum Curatrix
    holds up the small body
    of a sleeping woman runs her hand
    over the round lift of the hip

wind fills my ears with such stillness
all I can do is listen
to the echoing spill of the unheard

Notes by Curatrix

Going underground is an ancient tradition with us, but so too is building where the whole world lies at one's feet. Here at Mnajdra the wind caresses you, sometimes it almost knocks you over. The rocks hold the silence. We are elemental. But interrupting the silence is absurdity. I have been to see the curator at this museum. He was not friendly. I pointed out to him that Sumo wrestlers and earth goddesses hold the fat in their bodies in different areas. He would have none of it. Said his friend Colin knows best. In the exhibition space, Diana, Agnese and Sulpicia were making all the right noises and getting some of the other visitors to think critically about the signage. Two of the women began to chuckle. I think they had been on one of those goddess tours to Crete, Turkey or the Celtic lands, their eyes already able to see the disjunction. One by one change comes.

Lambda

six thousand years

you have to listen to this says Agnese
Curatrix showed me the web page
it's the sound of a six-thousand-year-old song
about sheep

> ... a sheep that had no wool saw horses, one of them pulling a
> heavy wagon, one carrying a big load, and one carrying a man
> quickly. The sheep said to the horses: "My heart pains me,
> seeing a man driving horses." The horses said: "Listen, sheep,
> our hearts pain us when we see this: a man, the master,
> makes the wool of the sheep into a warm garment for himself.
> And the sheep has no wool." Having heard this, the sheep fled
> into the plain.
>   – Schleicher's Fable (PIE: avis akvāsas ka) 1868

now she's found another

Lost text: PIE: sheep and the women
Proto-Indo-European, circa 6500 BP

I'd like to make a deal
says the head ewe

you've heard that story
about the sheep and the horses

the woman nods

well she blares
I don't mind sharing
just a little
but on my terms

what are your terms?

no shearing to begin
on the first day of winter
it's too damn cold

but says the woman
you don't want to get sunburnt

true
so I will share my wool with you
only at the equinoxes

one more thing
those horses you've been riding
that's okay but no carts

agree?

agreed says the woman

Notes by Curatrix

This is a variant version of a six-thousand-year-old story. That fable and this have been reconstructed from Proto-Indo-European sources (also called PIE). This version is updated from a prior reconstruction by German linguist, August Schleicher. 'Sheep and the women' reflects recent research revealing that women were key players in the invention of thread and the manufacture of clothing.

they came in ships

with horses
so many dead
those not dead

captured
I was enslaved
taken into service

temples became lupanaria
our enslavement
our sacred duty

reversals are all
it was Helena
stable girl stabularia

lifted from the hell of harlotry
to earthly mother of Constantine
and heavenly mother of the church

echoes of Rhea Silvia
Mary Magdalena
Acca Larentia

ecclesiastical disorders
         – and the words of women
            are monstrosities

iynx

that poor iynx was tortured
yoked to a four-spoked wheel
caught in eternal flight
her wings in mad rush of breath

iynx: Greek: Eurasian
wryneck (woodpecker),
Jynx torquilla

a lure for Medea
by unscrupulous Jason
      she catches her breath on bird wings
is caught yoked in marriage

a Jason jinx
the original fall
they fell one after the other
      Tiamat
      Medea
      Eve

craft

those who came after us
unravelled our stories
wiped the slate clean
smashed the pots
leaving only fragments

so we kept silent
we avoided the high arts
the public world
the official histories

craft saved us
        we spun and sewed
        wove patterns on fabric
        cooked and healed
        drew on pots
        sang and told old wives' tales
        to our daughters
        we were ignored
        we were inventive
        and we laughed

they call women monsters

I am a monster.
— Robin Morgan, *Monster*

breasts lined in rows
four rows of two
like the bitch she is
women breasts above
a gallimaufry of breasts

wings beat
to their own rhythm
that soaring eagle soul
talons catch the child spirit
who cannot live

claws morph eagle
to lion they tear flesh
tread the earth softly
roar in cub protection
big enough to tear you apart

this tail muscled
its end a frill of hair
will swipe you
her eyes do not sleep
her mane is unkempt

under the ocean's waves
another monster
captures pilgrims dives deep
spits Jonah from her mouth
renouncing her depths

a memory of
Madonna of the harpies
winged angels
clasp her calves
harpies support her feet

Medusa Gorgon Leviathan
Dragon Griffin Grendel
Echidna Hydra Striga
Lamia Charybdis Scylla
Amphisbaena Sphinx

minder of the lost texts: Angelic: Curatrix
2014 CE

in my Musæum Matricum
there remain many texts
not yet open to the public
and so much more to excavate

I'll be gathering stories
at Livia's party
where many tales will be told
in the meantime I have work to do

Livia's connections

Livia is well-connected
never shy of networking
she has the ear of bishops
cardinals even the pope

they have sent an emissary
inviting any who wish to visit
the Vatican Museum
to have drinks on the lawn

Diana says *I can bring my dogs*
Agnese says *will Papa show me his pallia*
Ceres says *they demonised my rituals*
Curatrix says *I can be the guide*

Livia is disappointed by these attitudes
she says *this new guy Francesco*
he's really trying to make things better
for all the marginalised ones

Curatrix sniffs *two thousand years too late*
I want our property returned
I want Diana of Ephesus in my Musæum
I want all the animals and all the women

La Donna Lupa
Paleolitica: Italian: the
Paleolithic she-wolf or
Paleolithic wolf-woman
(officially called La
Donna Lupo Paleolitico)

she continues *I want to excavate*
under these walls find the temple
to Demeter hidden there
invite La Donna Lupa Paleolitica

there is an uncomfortable silence
Livia is hurt by their refusals
but she has other things up her sleeve
I will come to your hotel and collect you

the cardinals have offered their cars
everyone looks to Ceres and Curatrix
well okay then we can be a modern
cavalcade as we enter the side way

Curatrix says *let's drink their coffee*
teas wine eat the cakes and pastries
but remember even this pope forgets
women are the poorest of the poor

Musæum Matricum

merriments abound as we amble
narrow streets searching for Musæum Matricum
in the heat everything rises the sun clasps you close
when you try to find your way out

Agnese is nostalgic for the past
god knows why it wasn't kind to her
but perhaps she is hoping for a gentler future
we enter the cool Musæum

Curatrix has everything here
rooms filled with our treasures
hidden for so long in the dark corners
of their neutered museums

winged ones wolves lions horses
even flying cows with shining mouths
I remember no fear in the lion's den
and there are no gilded cages

among them new works with names attached
cow heads by Georgia O'Keeffe Frida Kahlo stands
among butterflies Suzanne Bellamy's porcelain women
discuss astronomy with the old ones

over by the many-breasted ones
something luminous Minnie Pwerle's
painting of breasts in aquamarine orange
red yellow against a purple background

a crowd musters around the vulvals
the sheela-na-gigs Suzanne Santoro's paintings
dinner plates by Judy Chicago photos by Lariane
Fonseca and poets declaiming in loud voices

Agnese likes the past and the cool
but is spooked by mobs she grabs
Diana by the hand and heads for the door
stops in stupor at the Etruscan ewe's head

sheep have always been her undoing

hats

Hatshepsut leads the parade of hats
and hairdos that resemble hats
sun-haters wear wide-brimmed wonders
made of lace or grass or leaf stem
the odd fascinator standing out
purple feathers green and white trimmed

there are small hats made of felt
knitted woven patchworked
in sombre and bright colours
the stylish among them wear
cloches and fedoras
berets and boaters

some come swathed in veils and scarves
desert women arrive wearing
colourful beanies over their ears
farmers in akubras and hard hats
sombreros and panamas
and the dykes on bikes in helmets

as we enter all head coverings are removed
this is a place for women

tarantella

Livia's outdone herself
the room is alive
leaves shimmer in light
birds all a-twitter
luscious balls of fruit hanging

our favourite goddesses
appear as plants
quince brings luck in love
pomegranate binds love and death
poppy a favourite from Eleusis

Diana Venus and Ceres are dancing
in a circle with
Hecate Aphrodite and Demeter
the first triad from Roma
the second from Greek Sicilia

Cybele appears
wild iris entwined
in a pine branch procession
some women need pageantry
una processione femminile

una processione
femminile: Italian: a
procession of women

Diana why the ilex
is there something we should know?
others enter bearing
a veritable pharmacopoeia
from shrubs and herbs

the nieces of Sicilian Medusa
and a group of Maori girls
are trading tongue gestures
for now it is playful
but each knows how fear can kill

Olympias and Agave arm in arm
snake-braceleted maenads twirl dust storms
the world is a-whirl Psappha shouts
we are the ones I wrote about
someone in some future time will remember me

you can teach an old god new tricks

it is time
we reassert ourselves
from every continent
from many times
but the most numerous are the old ones
not just old
                    ancient
not just ancient
                    prehistoric
they come in tunics and saris
in wound cloths and in string skirts
they come in animal hides
and they come naked

they carry musical instruments and carpets
nulla nullas and digging sticks
spindles and pots
bowls and fans
some carry nothing at all
being in the habit of travelling light

La Donna Lupa Paleolitica
is naked but for a wolf mask
Mary has drifted aloft in the thermals
of mid-August heat it matters not
if she is Goodijalla ascending
or winged Nemesis or Isis
or any number of angelic
or harpic beings

Victoria is taking flight
from the wedding cake

nulla nulla: Dharuk: a
heavy club

Goodijalla: Djiru: sea
eagle

117

for an early breakfast with
Eos Uşas and local Aurora
who know all the best caffès in Roma
they lounge in sunlit chairs
refuse to pay the table service
excess

many breasted

the many-breasted ones are here in droves
from Roma comes Lupa in company
with harpies griffins and Egyptian phoenix
they howl and call like a rabble of banshees

from Ephesus Diana her many breasts
sweet as mangoes
as the ancient Tamil
poets would say

Livia welcomes them provides spritz
Aperol or Campari she asks
introduces them to a group of dust-red women
their breasts painted up

the women invite the old ones to dance with them
their easy shuffle raises the dust of the piazza
they dance to the sound of an ancient drone
and rising voices

look it's Psappha and her thiasos
come to join the dance their tender feet
there's a vibration in the air rarely felt these past
six thousand years

thiasos: Greek: school,
community, retinue,
followers

underground

Manastabal has taken over from Curatrix and says
always look for those who have to go underground
takes us to Calypso's cave in a cliff above the crashing Maltese sea
the hidden one whose hollow can be entered only on belly and thighs

before we know it we are stilled in the silence of the hypogeum
its skeletons humming and thrumming in that curled chamber
they are rushing us now Persephone Inanna Sarasvatī
clamouring over whose hideout is deepest who the darkest

Sarasvatī skites who else has a river named after them
an invisible line on a map Inanna is shepherding kings swathed
in seven veils she stomps around the fissured floor in frustration
Persephone sips red wine and nibbles seeds of winter pomegranates

Etruscans and Cretans are arguing about their necropoli and labyrinths
which was the most beautiful the Etruscan queen shows us her fresco
of dancing maenads drunk with desire at the hour of death
Ariadne meanwhile has found the centre and will not speak of it

Agnese is itching to show us her place the tufa maze under Rome
here sup seven women sharing bread she names them Saturnia
Hilarina Dominanda Rogatina Serotina Paulina Donata every one
a virgin and here Susanna defending herself against the charge of adultery

Manastabal leads us to one last concealed site music shudders through us
a long bar with an array of beverages from retsina and Latin wines
to whiskeys grappa beer the Queen of Wands beckons Wittig
and Judy Grahn calls *come have a drink what's your poison?*

Hotel Silvia

Hotel Silvia is full to the brim
its proprietrix
Rhea Silvia
has been preparing for months
the rooms are clean
sheets stretched
poppies on every bedside table
she has a line-up of acts ready for her guests
the like of which
has not been seen for several millennia
there are artists and poets
musicians and dramaturgs
aerialists and acrobats
jongleurs and jugglers
singers and percussionists

in Piazza Navona her boys
Romulus and Remus
have put up the marquee
laid the tables
set up the sound system for her favourite bands

ClitOris
Women's Electric Band
Nice Girls Don't Spit
Raylene Citizen and the Outskirts
and the yodelling twins
all from out of the way places
on the other side of the world

Santa Barbara and the heroine of
Roman sounding CMXL have teamed up
for some explosive fireworks

at the end a featured act called simply
Alix xx

performance poem by Curatrix: slut but but

I'm a slut
but but
ma non sono non sono
I'm a slot
I'm a slut
ma ma
ma che significa?
am I a slut?
but but
he said you're a slut
he said look at your butt
you're a slut
dicevo
but but
she said she's a slut
no buts about it
just a slut
all smut
tutti dicevano she's a slut
sicuramente
but but I said
I said but
I'm no slut
non sono una fessura per il tuo attrezzo
I'm not here for you
he said but but
no slut here
no fear
he said but but
she said but but
they said but but
I'm not the butt of your names
le tue parole non sono le mie parole

no fuckin way
chiudi il becco
I'm no slut
sto solo camminando
non sono una zoccola
so butt out
vattene dalla mia mente
I'll think what I want
I'll do what I want
I'll walk at 3 am if I want
indosserò stivaloni ci tirerò calci
porterò i capelli come mi pare
corti o lunghi
ma non farò sesso per strada
because I'm not here for you
tu sei uno stalker
cos I'm no slut
you say but but
you look like a slut
you must be a slut
if you're out at 3 am
if you don't look girlie
you must be a fuckin femminista
they're all sluts
that's what they are
and I say
you got it boy
you got it girl
sono una femminista
now fuck off

Notes by Curatrix

I don't plan to comment on this poem as it speaks for itself even if not every
word is known to you. You can find it on YouTube.

Hildegard

the abbesses making communion
share food drink ideas and
a fine choral alleluia for Ursula
and eleven thousand virgin companions

renunciates these nuns are unsullied
pure as paradise not for them
a covering veil the lovely vitality
of the virgin its own protection

separate and celibate
they have dragged themselves
into exile like doves without nests
all *for the sake of the lamb's embrace*

Pulcheria has pledged lifelong celibacy
inciting her sisters to join her
she's as excited as a beauty particle
in collision with all that matters

Santa Teresa in ecstasy over Hildegard's
refusenik compositions Saint Julian and kd
sing an ethereal duet their voices
as powerful as the trumpets of Jericho

wolf pack

wolves have come in a pack
leading them is Guadalupe
her shimmering rays a full body halo
as if Hildegard had drawn flaming petals around her
strains of mediaeval music mingle with Nahuatl
it's uncanny but like the halo it works

with full pageantry comes Virginia Woolf
dressed in an Ethiopian jalaba
instead of standing to attention
she reclines in a wicker chair smoking
declaiming the end of war

Christa Wolf bursts in bringing with her a trainload of workers
who carry banners with the word
PROLETARIAT written in red
Anna Wulf too has a banner
WORKERS OF THE WORLD UNITE
but it's torn and dragging along the ground
increasingly shredded with each step

Anna Wulf is carrying a book
shining as brightly as Guadalupe's halo

Guadalupe has her arm around quotidian Mary
they have begun to howl not worrying
that the moon is not in the right phase
it'll come says the second Mary
when we reach BE
elemental quintessential
that is what matters

in the distance a song
everyone turns the hags the fairies
the eldest ones all talk stops
they stand listen to this song at the edge of hearing

a very old woman joins the party
her bearing perfectly straight
feet as light as a bird
dust gusts rise turn spiral whisper away
build become willy-willies flirting with the land
air carries the song
the winds become women dancing

and then another
La Donna Lupa Paleolitica
wolf-woman
at 300 000 years she deserves respect
she says *I'm tired of museum life*
I want to return to the slow stream
rock time planet time

Vassar's young women crowd the wolves
a Marxist lesbian party gathers
around Christa and Anna
but Anna is leaving with her shining book
she's asking Virginia about form
the form itself
how to break through these limitations
Christa is leaving her party too
wanders over to where Medea is fixing
a wing on her serpented flying chariot
she always was competent

Anna lopes back to Guadalupe they are shouting
not in anger so much as excitement

you have to descend first says Guadalupe
I'll wait for you
a visionary can't avoid her visions no matter the horror
Virginia is nodding wishes she'd had
Guadalupe to hold her hand
at the time of her descents

Lupa and Medea are talking in the corner
the word 'sons' is overheard by Curatrix
why don't I teach them to speak Angelic?

there's a noise at the gate voices of a different timbre
a group of men is shouting their weapons visible
Diana Hippolyta Minerva and a crush of Amazons
bar their way they bear no arms
but there's that no-nonsense stance

then the martyrs step forward
you don't scare us any more
put down your weapons

the burly ones are like puppies and do as they are told
a group of suits are betting on the outcome
money is changing hands too quickly
to see what currency they are using

Agnese is speechifying
you have work to do
and it won't be done
by standing there calling us names
telling us you've been hurt
see my scars she raises her shirt
shows the burn marks
points to the scar across her throat
if you want to know hurt

look at every woman here
the bravest and the oldest
both rich and poor bear scars

go on one of Anna Wulf's descents
if you must
but right now you have to leave
and work on those money changers
the temples have become banks
the banks temples
it's your turn to fix it

she turns and walks away

the men stand dumbfounded
some are angry say they should rape us
teach us a thing or two all over again
but a few de-escalate

Barbara reminds the weaponed ones
she's their saint the one in charge of explosives
she suggests to the mathematicians at the back
that they owe her too and perhaps they could get started
on convincing the chargers of interest
the forgers of currencies
that money is as abstract as calculus
more illusory than an imaginary number
and more irrational
you can't take it with you

they break off into groups
begin to talk
they've a bit of ground to cover
so let's leave them at their own party
they can send us an emissary when they are ready

Lost text: Lupine: La Donna Lupa Paleolitica

circa 300 000 BP

read me
from the feet up
the lower levels rise
all is descent

my legs and thighs
are scored by time
I am scarred sacred
never scared

my mound of Venus
you shamefully call pudenda
the triangle inverted
calyx at its centre

on my belly small rings
counting moon days
arms crossed
x doubled

above my breasts
I wear a pendant
at the point from which
you can hear me growl

when you look up
you'll see my wolfish head
ears alert for sound
nose scanning scent

turn me over
my companion Loba
beside me and the rest
of the pack behind

Notes by Curatrix

Livia invited La Donna Lupa Paleolitica to the party because, at 300 000 years, she's the oldest known wolf-woman in existence. And her current home in an unmarked back room at the museum in Ancona means she will not be missed for some time. She says she is happy there among the flinty rocks, but now and then she misses woman companionship. *Thank goodness for my friend, Loba*, she sighs.

friendship among women

it is said
that Salome gave great gifts
of land to Livia
that wealth creates more wealth
and power the same
it was in friendship that these gifts
were given
what we hear is only the nastiness
of Livia
and Salome's naked dance

at the party Cleopatra
bearded Hatshepsut
and the marvellous Queen of Sheba
who in Rome
has a church called San Saba
her names
are numerous and varied
Balquis Nakuti Malkeda
Oloye Bilikisu Sungbo say the Yoruba

Dido is singing her way through
the latest
operatic version of her disastrous
love
Boudicca charges
in on her horse apologising for
being late
it's a long way from the Apple Isle
she chides

though they be mere mortals
these women
are equal in character to gods
they led peoples
had the faults of humans
they changed
history they challenged the order
of things

tomb of the forgotten women

there is nothing here
       but silence

we begin to sing
we chant the names
of some who tried
to end their enslavement

Abigail Allecto Amy Andrea Angela
Anna Anne Asja Betty Carla Carole
Caroline Carolyn Catharine
Christine Chyng Cloti Coleen Diane
Elise Elizabeth Finola Gail Giti Helen
Inga Janice Julia Kajsa Kat Kathleen
Kaye Lara Lee Linda Lise Liza
Mangai Mary Meagan Melinda
Melissa Monique Naparulla Natalie
Ninotchka Olivera Patricia
Powhiri Queenie Rachel Rebecca
Renate Ritu Robin Robyn Ruchira
Sheila Stella Stephanie Susan
Suzanne Terry Urvashi Vednita Vicky
Wendy Xena Yoko Zohl

Agatha Agnese Anastasia
Artemisia Balbina Barbara
Baubo Cecilia Demeter Diana
Dimitra Donna Lupa Eurosia Felice
Giovanna Hecate Ilia Lucia
Penthesileia Rhea Silvia Susanna Ursula

the chant continues and could go on
for days months years eons
Lilla says *the future extends*
as far forward as the past

we have millennia ahead

Demeter and Santa Dimitra

some have dual citizenship
saints and goddesses
demons and goddesses
witches and goddesses

witches and saints
the line all a-blur
the statue of Demeter
say her acolytes

was worshipped longer than any other
in the entire world
some don't build statues but we won't enter
that old argument

about hemispheres and empire
Demeter's newer partner is Santa Dimitra
together they have taken on not just Olympus
but the whole theistic edifice

they speak of molestation abduction rape
the Loeb version says poor Persephone was
    rapt away
    given to Hades by all-seeing Zeus

rapt away?
he had no business
that upstart from the Idaean cave
Persephone's mother heard the child's cry

in her heart and with dark cloak of wings flew
across the land seeking her

but all refused to speak
they said they didn't know

Demeter has the floor she says
even Helios who told the truth
thought he could cajole me with
blandishments and offers of honour

as slippery as Romulus trading Roman
citizenship for Sabine shame
they knew me in Etruria
moulded statues hid them away

underground well-packed in soil
they covered me allowed the moss
to grow over my lips
only I remembered my name

in what is called the Classical Period
– with capitals –
everyone visited her sanctuary
at Eleusis at least once in a lifetime

Demeter looks at Livia shifts focus
she says *you are all a soft touch*
you took the offerings went to headquarters
for cakes coffee tea and drinks!

I hung myself out to dry for months
not speaking in a wrath of grief
refusing wine and bread
drinking only barley water

I vowed not to enter the halls of Olympus
with its flowers and fruits on eternal offer

not until my daughter was returned to me
I would have let them all starve

Persephone came back but not before
another betrayal with winter seeds
the people in this place remembered
the rites I taught them at Eleusis

Livia is nodding others too
still secret after all this time
the peasants knew the saint
sister Dimitra kept them safe

kept their fields fertile
Demeter resumes her old name
fills the space with her presence
they are destroying me yet again

as if it wasn't enough that they build
a soap factory over my shrine
after the soap factory
a fertilizer plant

what do they think we were doing all
those thousands of years?
fertilizer was in our rites
we protected the soil

they propitiated me
I kept them budding
after the fertilizer came the pesticides
is Rachel here? thank goodness for your work

it was a close call with DDT
those endlessly innovative brains

have concocted something even worse
GMO – should I spell that out

caps again please –
Genetically Modified Organisms
anyone with half a brain and some experience
in conception fertility and maternity

can see that if you make them all the same
it is a DISASTER – turn off those caps
if you overdo it no one will listen
the space is completely silent

and what do they do?
homogenise globalise one size fits all
Vandana Farida seed collectors
this is what I should have done

instead of anointing him with ambrosia
and breath of immortal fire
I should have taught Demophoön
the gentle art of collecting seed

future unbuilt

a circle has formed
not in Livia's sunken garden
but in the olive grove
with its harvest of poppies
about to break through

the desert women are talking
with the old ones from Sardegna
they speak of the unbuilt environment
intangible space
how earth provides
Nganyintja draws a map of circles
across the land
shows how these unbuilt places
are linked by song

Farida from Bangladesh joins them
they've moved on to the subject
of uncultivated plants

there's a sudden rush of opinions
from all the old ones
women of the snowy lands
forests and deserts
Minangkabau Mosuo Khasi
Wiradjuri Aranda Djiru

the Africans and the Sami
Irish and the Yemeni
the Indians and Europeans
the island nations too
all have something to say about

herbs and vegetables
fruits grains fungi
roots barks and seeds

the unbuilt and the uncultivated
could keep this planet alive

Eleonora d'Arborea

she sails in from Sardegna
with a falcon on her wrist
a bird's nest in her hair
she brings her fourteenth-century
scrolls and laws
protecting the rights of women

Mary Wollstonecraft puts her arm
around her shoulder
carefully avoiding the falcon

following the discussion of the unbuilt
the old ones have talked through three nights
and along with Susan B Vida G and Eleanor R
have made ready a new universal
declaration not just of human rights
but the rights of the planet and all
who live here

details are examined
rewritten by poets and editors
wrangled and written again
discussed and turned over
the wording careful
they've all seen
unexpected consequences before

by sunrise
everyone at this party has had a say
the final draft will be written up
and handed out
at moonrise

panthea

the bus pulls up
at the Pantheon
Ceres Demeter
and Santa Dimitra
are discussing
how they should
initiate these new women

Santa Dimitra
is for a wild dance
but Ceres
comes with visions
in her pocket

whispers
stalks of rye
cogito ergot *sum*
wolf's tooth
sporal magic
a cornucopia
of chances

barley wolf
baying and howling
hallucinations
shining mysteries
our histories

in bocca alla lupa
viva la lupa

in bocca alla lupa: Italian
(variant of in bocca al
lupo): in the mouth of
the she-wolf; good luck

viva la lupa: Italian: long
live the she-wolf

143

manitari

there was a time when
we called the sky
Eos Uşas Aphrodite
Astarte Ishtar Isis

of course of course
and those others
Circe Calypso Arianrhod
Medea Semele

all who came from
sea sun and moon
gleaming silver and golden
in their beauty

those names those names
a chant
slipped into as the syllables
fall from my tongue

manitari (μανιταρι):
Modern Greek:
mushroom

manitari ambrosia amṛta
food for immortals
little golden
breast-like

pearl gleaming
your silver stalks
extended
in welcome

144

Baubo

the hours of talk were long
and they have agreement

Baubo is leading a morning ritual
she is flanked by Demeter and Medusa
it begins as a low belly rumble
releases into a wide open laugh

laughter ricochets around the circle
infecting each one of us
Baubo makes Demeter laugh again
Medusa laughs her head off

La Befana is running around
with her other half Perchta
handing out honeyed figs and dates

their broomsticks are for
sweeping the sky
not sweeping floors

we laugh at our pain
we laugh to stay sane

seized

she writes this poem
as a prophylactic
against loss and darkness
descents are many
she travels
like a particle
along two paths
one a tendency towards existence
sense and memory
the other towards non-existence
nonsense and annihilation
she carries the energies
of a dark universe
visions of an underworld
long past and rising
she is the lamb in the sheepfold
wolf in the forest
virgin violated
lupa levitated
madonna whore
lesbian lover
her transitoriness
is as permanent
as memory and invention
she falls and rises falls and rises
like a wave

sibyls

Phemonoe the poet
says it is time to cease
prophesying

the future is now
time is
turned on itself

there
        then
here
        now

the known a memory
the knowable invented
our million mouths singing

the calculus of lambda (λ)

the variable x is a valid lambda term
what of xx
a valid identity?

lambda calculus solves my world
points to another lambda
and the dark energy driving the universe

or quintessence?

if t and s are lambda terms
then (ts) is a lambda term

calculus is about discovering the unknown
let us discover a universe in which lambda
is knowable

the observations click
purple shift
that emotional leap of faith into other realms
a transit out of time into timelessness

> *where*
> x = woman
> t = transit
> s = you work it out

A note on dates

BP: Before Present
aC: Avanti Cristo (Italian): Before Christ
BCE: Before Common Era (used in place of BC)
CE: Common Era (used instead of AD: Anno Domini)
BE: Biophilic Era

Background notes by Curatrix

3. descent
Medusa: One of three Gorgon sisters who are powerful winged daemons (Greek: benevolent spirits). The other two are immortal and named Stheno and Euryale. The Gorgons are associated with birds, snakes, sows and sometimes have short beards (like goats). Medusa was the only mortal among them and in a story reminiscent of the later virgin martyrs, King Polydectes orders Perseus to fetch her head. He decapitates her.

4. canis
Canicula, in the constellation Canis Major (The Big Dog), is the brightest star in the sky and has been known by many names: Canicula to the Romans and Σείριος Seirios: 'glowing' or 'scorcher' (Latinised Sirius) to the ancient Greeks.

The heliacal rising of Canicula 2000 years ago marked the beginning of what the ancients called the dies caniculares or 'dog days'. Because the precession of the equinoxes takes around 26 000 years, in the Roman period and at Rome's latitude it would be just over a month earlier than it rises now. The 'dog days' at that time were early July, and as the Greek word indicates, it is the hottest time of the year.

The story of Romulus and Remus probably has its origins among the Etruscans.

Artemisia Gentileschi (1593–c.1656): Roman Baroque painter. One of the few women of the period whose work survives. Anna Banti's novel, *Artemisia*, explores the repercussions of a rape trial of which she was the victim. One of her most famous paintings is *Judith Slaying Holofernes* (1611–1612).

Socrates (470/469–399 BCE): *The Symposium* by Plato records a discussion by Socrates and others about the nature of love at a drinking party. This is philosophy!

5. throw me to the wolves
Venus: Roman goddess of love, equivalent of Greek Aphrodite.

9. hop-on hop-off bus
Costanza: the 4th-century church of Santa Costanza was built by Emperor Constantine in honour of his daughter Constantina (also known as Constantia or Costanza) who died in 354 CE.

10. tour of the lost texts
Curatrix is guardian of the invisible doorway to the past; her native language is Angelic, related to Phoenician, Tocharian, Lesbian, and Lydian.

Musæum: The library of Alexandria housed many texts and probably some of the Lost Texts. Next door to it was the Musæum: a place of food, pleasure, and intellectual debate.

A poet or artist: Suzanne Bellamy's performance work, The Lost Culture of Women's Liberation paved the way for a new kind of research.

Marija Gimbutas and James Mellaart are the two best known exponents of contextual archaeology.

11. Lost text: Ooss: dog three bones has
This text was discovered at the Mongarlowe Studio, NSW, and translated by Curatrix at Suzanne Bellamy's place in December 2011.

Suzanne Bellamy says of her work, 'This artwork of text/image fusion is constructed with a variety of handmade porcelain shapes and metal objects arranged on a painted surface inside a wooden box. My text box series explores ideas about embedded language and meaning, in this case in relation to poetic structures, surface tension, punctuation, eye movement, and the irresistible urge to create meaning. I invited my poet and linguist friend to "translate" the box as a form of surrealist experiment in "making it real". Her poem and notations thus become one of many possible translation experiments.'

The original artwork can be found on the back cover of this book.

13. what Lupa says
Aurora: Roman goddess of dawn.

In 2011, archaeologists reported finding a holy shrine to Demeter near Viterbo, 80 kilometres north of Rome. It contains Etruscan votive offerings dating back to at least 1000 BCE.

16. nuraghe
The island of Sardinia (Italian: Sardegna) is known for its Bronze Age structures, conical towers built of dry stone, called nuraghe (Italian: pl. nuraghi). The people of Sardinia began constructing these buildings around 1800 BCE and continued until about 600 BCE when the island was conquered by the Carthaginians. Sardinia also has pre-Nuragic structures including megalithic circles, menhirs and the tantalising breasted baetyls. Some baetyls were meteorites.

Iynx was a nymph who administered magic love potions, one of which she offered Zeus, who then fell in love with Io. Instead of Zeus being punished for his infidelity, a furious Hera turned Iynx into a bird: the wryneck.

Colossal stone: there are numerous stories from Sardinia, Scotland, Malta and elsewhere in Europe about women – some carrying spindles, some breastfeeding – who toss huge stones thereby changing the landscape, build gigantic structures overnight or before breakfast.

20. Ilia's dream
This poem is translated from the Latin poem by Ennius written in 150 BCE.

Ilia/Rhea Silvia is the daughter of Aeneas (responsible for founding the city of Rome after the Cumaean Sibyl's prophecy) and Eurydice; she is the full sister of the unnamed woman whom she addresses in this poem. Ilia is the mother of Romulus and Remus, the children born as a result of the rape by the god of war, Mars.

Ilia's alternative name is Rhea Silvia. Rhea resembles the Greek word rheo 'flow', therefore associated with the river, the spirit of the Tiber. It is possible there is a connection to res and regnum, hence to the ruling family. Silvia is the Latin word for 'forest' or 'woods', suggesting a goddess of the forests, perhaps Diana.

This story has so many convolutions because Ilia aka Rhea Silvia is also a vestal virgin. The vestal virgins were selected at a very young age (six to ten years) and expected to remain virgins until the age of thirty-five. In a society where a virgin is an independent woman with sacred power, the important thing is that she not be at the beck and call of a husband. By being selected, this daughter of royalty is prevented from producing direct heirs. Her father Numitor had a nasty younger brother, Amulius, who had already killed Numitor's son and wanted to see an end to his line. In the poem Ilia is referred to as a daughter of Aeneas (eleven generations back), a shorthand term representing the lineage of Aeneas.

When Rhea Silvia aka Ilia gave birth to twins the punishment was jail (weighed down with chains, according to Livy) and her children thrown in the river. They survive because they were set beside the river and found by the shepherd, Faustulus.

22. Lupa's story
Lupa, the she-wolf, inhabits the hills of the Palatine, possibly the site of an earlier Etruscan sacred site. The Palatine is one of the seven sacred hills of Rome. In among the ancient pink walls is a small shrine with no signs to indicate anything of importance. In the shrine is a bird-wolf-woman and, on a lower level, a sheep's head.

24. Sabine women
The rape of the Sabine women is what one might call an apocryphal story. The standard version states that everything turned out all right in the end. But it is told from the point of view of Romulus who ordered the rape; the men of Rome who perpetrated the rape; the winners' tale.

27. diary of a vestal virgin

The Vestal Virgins continued to have power in Classical Rome. They paid no taxes, were the only ones allowed to drive a cart through the Forum (Senators did not share this privilege), and had the best seats in the Colosseum, near the Emperor.

The vestal virgin's job was to keep alight the flame in the Temple of Vesta. Vesta was the goddess of hearth and home (Hestia in Greece). If the fire went out, Rome's end was near. This Roman temple was originally built around the eighth century BCE.

The fire of the vestals was extinguished by order of Christian Emperor Theodosius I in 394 CE. The College of the Vestals was then disbanded, but an interesting side story is the appropriation of the vestals' garments by the church. The main items of clothing of a vestal were an infula (white and red woollen fillet), a suffibulum (white and purple woollen veil), and a palla (long, very simple shawl made of wool which Roman women wore as everyday clothing). When a Catholic priest attains the status of cardinal he receives a woollen item of clothing. The Pope wears a pallium.

29. drama queens

Like theatre women in many cultures, natī are sometimes regarded as lupa. A natī is an older, more knowledgeable woman, one who is versed in the language and its history. She combines the voice of the actress in the Prologue and that of a mother/mentor for the three young women: Śakuntalā and her sakhī (sahī).

30. Lost text: Śaurasenī and Mahārāṣṭrī Prakrits: Sahīo, a drama

The Prakrits are the languages spoken by women and 'inferior characters' in drama. It is likely that the speakers of Sanskrit (men of the upper caste, Brahmins) and speakers of Prakrit (women and lower castes) saw the world rather differently. In this translation, the word Prakrtī is used with a long ī, as a way of indicating the female-centredness of the imagery, except when Natī refers to Prakrits (plural) where the English spelling is used. Also worth noting is that prākrt means low, vulgar, unrefined, original and any provincial or vernacular dialect cognate with Sanskrit.

34. salone

Women have a history of creating salons: spaces where literary, political and intelligent conversation is practised. The salon was an Italian invention of the sixteenth century where Isabella d'Este possibly held the first. They became very popular in France and in the twentieth century Natalie Barney and Gertrude Stein excelled at the art of the salon. In Melbourne, Australia, Salon-A-Muse was a monthly feminist salon that ran from 1982 to 1985.

The quotation from Joanna Russ is from the book's front cover.

35. Sulpicia i–vi

The Latin text for the translations (and variations) of Sulpicia's poems i–vi are taken from 'Epistulae'.

Sulpicia iv: stola: respectable women in Roma after the second century BCE were expected to wear stolas, whereas men wore togas. To distinguish them from respectability, prostitutes wore togas as well.

39. Latin: Sulpicia vii

Catullus, Roman poet, c.84 BCE–54 BCE.

44. Psappha in slippers

Psappha/Sappho was a poet, born between 630 and 612 BCE on Lesbos, off the coast of modern-day Turkey. She died around 570 BCE. Psappha invented lyric poetry and the myxolydian musical mode, and wrote in Aeolic Greek.

46. Diana shears Livia's flock

entre chien et loup: a French phrase which literally means 'between dog and wolf'. It refers to the time we call dusk, twilight or gloaming when the outlines of things can't be properly distinguished: is it a dog or a wolf? domestic or wild?

The Greek word lukophos (λυκόφωσ) means twilight, while lukauges (λυκαυγέσ) means dawn. Both come from the Greek word lukos (λύκοσ) which means wolf.

52. edī and avidugdha

The comparisons made here between the fleeces of sheep and clouds are readily seen, even by children, and in Sanskrit not only sheep but other animals are compared with clouds. For example, the sentiment expressed by a Yakṣa 'he saw an elephant cloud rutting the cliff face' can be found in Kālidāsa's poem Meghadūta.

Giti Thadani documents the frequent destruction of images of female deities, including the smashing, de-breasting and desecration of goddess statues (Thadani 2004: pp. 27–47). If the destruction of the Barmiyan Buddhas could not bring those destroyers to heel, what chance has a tiny poem about sheep?

55. the world according to Santa Barbara

La Barbe d'Action Féministe in France protests against discrimination and other inequalities through humour and the donning of fake beards.

The word 'barbarian' is said to come from a xenophobic joke that those speaking another language sound as though they are saying bar-bar or perhaps baa-baa. There is a similar story in Sanskrit in which the Mleccha are people who sound as though they are vomiting when they speak.

Barbara was the daughter of a rich trader, called Dioscorus. Because of her association with lightning, Barbara is the patron saint of military engineers, armourers, miners, artillerymen, and those who work with explosives; also of mathematicians.

58. come to kill us
In the early Christian church, the lamb was a more important symbol than Jesus as a baby.

The pallium is worn only by the Pope. It is made from the wool of white lambs bred especially for this purpose. The lambs are raised by nuns from the convent of Santa Agnese and the wool woven into pallia by the nuns from the Benedictine church of Santa Cecilia in Trastevere.

Vestal Virgins wore a palla over the left shoulder and guarded the Palladium, an object of worship providing safety to the person holding it. There is a depiction on a Pompeii fresco in the atrium of the Casa del Menandro of this rule of safety, asylum, and refuge being broken, as Cassandra is hauled away from the Trojan Palladium into slavery.

Santa Cecilia (died c.180 CE): The Roman state's persecution of women – or indeed girls, as many were aged twelve to seventeen – was full of hatred for women's independence of thought and action. Cecilia was forced into marriage. First her tormentors stoned her then tried to suffocate her in the steam of a sudatorium. This failed and a decapitation was attempted, but her head was not fully severed and she lay dying for three days. Another version says Cecilia continued singing after she was beheaded. She is the patron saint of music and musicians; a kind of Orpheus figure.

The church of Santa Cecilia is in Trastevere, first built in the third century.

62. Lost text: Kartvelian: Medea's lambs
Kartvelian is the language of Colchis, the home of Medea.
Little Iliad: a lost epic about the Trojan War, probably written in the seventh century BCE. Thirty lines of the original text survive.

64. Sant' Angela di Merici on the precative
Angela di Merici was born in Lombardy in 1474. When she was fifteen, her older sister, Gianna, died suddenly without receiving the sacraments. Angela increased her prayers and received a vision that her sister was in heaven surrounded by saints. At the age of twenty, she began to teach girls in her home, believing they needed better education. Later she set up an association of virgins who would devote themselves to the education of girls.

65. Joan and the Johns
The dates of Pope Joan (La Papessa Giovanna) are disputed. This is not surprising since she is also omitted from the official list of Popes. Some say 1099, while novelist Donna Woolfolk Cross uses the dates 814–855 CE.

67. the calculus of umbrals
Umbral calculus refers to a method of working out equations in which pretending that something is the case helps to solve the equation. It is considered a shadowy technique for 'proving' solutions.

The italicised words in the poem are taken from Pope Benedict XVI.

The spirals in the church of San Clemente resemble the spirals on the stonework of neolithic temples at Tarxien and Ġgantija in Malta.

75. Domitilla and Priscilla
In the catacombs of Priscilla, God is depicted as a bird.

77. crimes of women
Prostitutes, lupe, and so many of the female Christian martyrs were part of what Mary Daly (1984) calls 'the touchable caste'; those women whom men desire to touch, 'to have sexual intercourse with', 'to lay violent hands on'.

78. Sicilia: Santa Felicita
The body of Santa Felicita lies in the church of Santa Teresa alla Kalsa in Palermo.

79. Carthage, Tunisia: Santa Perpetua
There are arguments about dates of Santa Perpetua's death with some putting it at 203 CE. What is not in dispute is the authorship by Perpetua of her first-person account which details her visions. It is one of the earliest works by a Christian female writer to have survived. Her account is bolstered by an eyewitness who records her death.

80. Lost text: Akkadian: if I were booty
In memory of Eriste-Aye (c.1790–1745 BCE). Women need not commit crimes to be imprisoned and sometimes the prisons are called cloisters. Eriste-Aye was the daughter of the Akkadian king, Zimri-Lim. The original poem was translated by Willis Barnstone.

85. Tuscany: Il Giardino dei Tarocchi
Niki de Saint Phalle had a vision for the Tarot Garden, situated near the border of Umbria and Tuscany. She spent almost twenty years, from 1979 to 1998, building the site and its huge sculptural works, along with many other artists.

87. Lesbos: aidos
Aidos (αιδοσ) is the feeling one has when you want to speak but aidos (shame) stops you. Psappha writes about aidos in her fragment 137.

89. Lost text: Linear A: twenty-seven wethers
The vocabulary for this text has been taken from: Younger, J. 2013.

94. Malta: hypogeum
The only known prehistoric underground temple in the world is found on Malta at Hal-Saflieni.

102. Lost text: PIE: sheep and the women
'The Sheep and the Horses' also known as Schleicher's Fable.

Andrew Byrd, a contemporary linguist from the University of Kentucky has produced a sound file (Powell, 2014).

104. they came in ships
Helena (c.250–c.330 CE): stable girl, mother of Roman Emperor Constantine. Santa Helena's relics lie in the Basilica di Santa Maria in Aracoeli al Campidoglio, Roma.

107. they call women monsters
'Madonna of the Harpies' painted by Andrea del Sarto for the Convent of San Francesco dei Macci in Florence (1517; Florence, Uffizi).

110. Livia's connections
Diana of Ephesus: The Temple of Artemis (Greek Diana) was said, by Antipater of Sidon, to outshine all the other wonders of the ancient world. According to Callimachus (310/305–240 BCE), it was built by the Amazons. The Temple is situated about 75 kilometres south of the Turkish city, Izmir. While the temple has been destroyed, statues to Diana of Ephesus were made in the Hellenic period and can be found in museums such as the Musei Capitolini in Roma.

La Donna Lupa Paleolitica: dated to 300 000 BP (before present), this artifact is held in the Museo Archeologico Nazionale delle Marche in Ancona.

Ceres: Roman grain goddess, from whose name the word cereal is derived. In Greece, she is known as Demeter.

112. Musæum Matricum
There is an ancient poetic tradition of mentioning one's artistic ancestors and contemporaries. In the last chapter of Book 1 *Amores*, Ovid lists his literary forebears, mentors and colleagues: Homer, Hesiod, Callimachus, Sophocles, Aratus, Menander, Ennius, Accius, Varro, Lucretius, Virgil, Tibullus, and Gallus.

Suzanne Bellamy's porcelain women: a reference to Suzanne Bellamy's 'Buried Women's Army'. The astronomers refer to porcelain women in 'Observing and Documenting the Transit of Patriarchy', also by Suzanne Bellamy.

115. tarantella
Diana, Venus and Ceres are the equivalent Roman goddesses of the Sicilian trio of Hecate, Aphrodite and Demeter.

Cybele is the Anatolian Mother Goddess in Rome, known as Magna Mater.

Olympias and Agave are remembered because they were queens and mothers: Olympias, the mother of Alexander the Great; and Agave, mother of Pentheus. Both have come down to us as murderers and as women who practised nocturnal chthonic rituals. Perhaps the murderous tradition is a kind of ancient marketing. Agave is renowned for being the leader of the maenads in Euripides' play, *The Bacchae*, who collectively tore apart the man who came to spy on their rituals, Agave's son, Pentheus. Olympias is recalled for killing several members of her own family in disputes over claims to the Macedonian throne. She was executed without a hearing in 316 BCE.

117. you can teach an old god new tricks
Victoria: Roman goddess of victory, originally the Sabine goddess of agriculture, Vacuna. A temple was dedicated to her on the Palatine Hill.

Nemesis: Greek goddess of revenge or retribution, from Greek nemein: to give what is due.

Isis: Egyptian goddess of magic, agricultural fertility and motherhood. Isis became an important deity in Rome only to have a major temple, which lies under the Musei Capitolini, destroyed in 48 BCE. There were a number of temples to Isis in Rome.

Eos, Uṣas and Aurora are all goddesses of dawn: Eos in Homeric Greece; Uṣas in Vedic India; Aurora in Rome.

120. underground
Manastabal is the guide Monique Wittig uses in her revisionary rewriting of Dante's *Inferno*, in her novel, *Across the Acheron* (1987).

Persephone: Greek Queen of the Underworld. Abducted by Hades, mourned by Demeter. She is tricked into eating the seeds of the pomegranate, thereby ensuring she must return to the Underworld for half of every year.

Inanna: Sumerian goddess of love and fertility who makes a descent to the Underworld ruled by her sister, Ereshkigal. Stripped of her power, Inanna is turned into a corpse and hung on a meat hook for three days.

Sarasvatī: Hindu goddess of writing, knowledge, the arts and nature. The Sarasvatī River is reputed to run invisibly underground.

125. Hildegard
From the lyrics of Spiritui Sancto:

Spiritui sancto honor sit / qui in mente Ursule virginis / virginalem turbam / velut columbas collegit. // Unde ipsa patriam suam / sicut Abraham reliquit. / Et etiam propter amplexionem Agni / desponsiatonem viri sibi / abstraxit.

I can't better this translation by Kathryn Bumpass:

Honor to the Holy Spirit, / who, in the mind of the / virgin Ursula gathered a / throng of virgins like doves. // And she left her own country / just as Abraham did. / And she also tore herself away from / her pledge to a man for the sake / of the Lamb's embrace.

Hildegard was very taken by the story of Ursula and wrote thirteen works in her honour. Santa Ursula and 11 000 companions, all virgins, were slaughtered. When Ursula refused the king's hand, he shot her with an arrow. Caravaggio has a painting of this event which hangs in Naples at the Galleria di Palazzo Zevallos Stigliano.

Pulcheria: Proclaimed Augusta (Empress) at age fifteen, she was wonderfully single-minded. In 414 CE she pledged to remain celibate her whole life: not only that, but she insisted her sisters make the same pledge. While this was done as a statement of Christian asceticism, it is reminiscent of the Roman pagan tradition of Vestal Virgins, and the feminist term, 'wilful virgin'. Pulcheria's name means beauty and she ruled for forty years.

126. wolf pack
Anna Wulf: is a character in Doris Lessing's *The Golden Notebook*.

La Donna Lupa Paleolitica: is currently housed in the Museo Archeologico Nazionale delle Marche in Ancona.

134. tomb of the forgotten women
The Homeric Hymn to Demeter contains a long list of names of Greek goddesses. My lists of names throughout are an echo of this tradition as well as of the work of Monique Wittig, especially *The Guérillères* (1972). Diane di Prima's *Loba* (1978) also includes lists of names.

Here is the list which appears in lines 418–423 from *The Homeric Hymn to Demeter*, spoken by Persephone (Rayor, 2004):

> All of us were playing in a charming meadow:
> Leukippa, Phaino, Elektra, Ianthe,
> Melita, Iakha, Rhodeia, Kallirhoa,
> Melobosis, Tukhe, blossoming Okuroa,
> Khryseis, Ianeira, Akasta, Admeta,
> Rhodopa, Plouto, charming Kalypso,
> Styx, Ourania, lovely Galaxaura
> battle-rousing Athena, arrow-flinging Artemis.

Lilla: Lilla Watson said in 1984 of Aboriginal history, that *the future extends as far forward as the past. That means*, she said, *a 40 000-year plan*. As the poem indicates, there are many more names than will fit on this page or into this book.

136. Demeter and Santa Dimitra

Demeter is the subject of the *Homeric Hymn to Demeter*, and her sanctuary at Eleusis was one of the most important sacred places in the ancient world. Everyone who was anyone went there to be initiated, including Empress Livia. The rites were secret on punishment of death. Santa Dimitra is the Christianised version, which of course meant abandoning the rites and taking on Christian attributes.

they knew me in Etruria: a reference to the recently discovered statue of Demeter, now displayed in the Museo Archeologico Nazionale in Viterbo.

Emily Dickinson in poem 177 (449) wrote: Until the Moss had reached our lips – / And covered up – our names – .

Farida and Vandana: I am indebted to Farida Akhter of UBINIG in Bangladesh for her work on uncultivated plants, her wonderful seed collections, and much more. And to Vandana Shiva for her global activism on ecology.

140. future unbuilt

Nganyintja: at the Women and Labor Conference in 1984, Nganyintja taught me much about the importance of understanding the power of the group and how to support the weakest member with integrity.

142. Eleonora d'Arborea

Eleanora d'Arborea (1347–1404): Sardinian judge (officially regent) of Arborea, an independent part of Sardinia with Oristano its biggest city, she won a war and negotiated a favourable treaty with the Aragonese. In 1395 she wrote the Carta de Logu, a series of laws which protected the rights of women. They remained in place until they were overturned for the worse in 1827. Eleonora was also a keen ornithologist and wrote laws to protect falcons.

Mary Wollstonecraft (1759–1797), author of *A Vindication of the Rights of Woman* (1792).

Susan B: Susan B Anthony (1820–1906). Nineteenth-century American feminist who was hugely influential in bringing forward the suffrage movement in the USA.

Vida G: Vida Goldstein (1869–1949). Australian feminist and suffragist who fought for women's equality in both the state of Victoria and the nation. She was the first woman to stand for the Senate in the 1903 national election. She failed in this and other attempts (probably due to her pacifism during war), but her international reputation extended to both the UK and USA where she gave speeches heard by thousands.

Eleanor R: Eleanor Roosevelt (1884–1962): She oversaw the drafting of the Universal Declaration of Human Rights in 1951.

143. panthea
in bocca alla lupa: Italian: a variation on the Italian phrase in bocca al lupo: good luck. 'In the mouth of a wolf' is a reference to the mother wolf who picks up her cubs in her mouth and takes them to safety. The masculinisation of female activities including that of lupe/she-wolves is at work here.

Ergot is a fungus that grows on different kinds of grain, including barley, wheat, rye and paspalum. It is possible this was the substance in the sacred kykeon, consumed during religious rituals such as the Eleusinian mysteries which were performed in honour of Demeter.

145. Baubo
Baubo: when Demeter is in mourning for Persephone, Baubo makes Demeter laugh by raising her skirt and showing her genitals.

La Befana: the tradition of La Befana is strong in Italy, where an old woman on a broomstick brings sweets to children on 6 January. It is likely she is a version of the Sabine/Roman goddess Strina/Strenia. A similar Germanic tradition exists around the figure of Perchta.

147. sibyls
In Greek mythology, Phemonoe was a poet of the pre-Homeric era. She is credited with inventing the poetic meter, the hexameter. Phemonoe was a priestess at Delphi and is identified by Servius as the Cumaean Sibyl. Sibyls were women with oracular powers whose prophesies were regarded as possessing great importance.

148. the calculus of lambda (λ)
Lambda-cold dark matter model (ΛCDM model) is the currently preferred and simplest model of the universe that best fits with observations; this model includes the Big Bang and the parameter lambda associated with dark energy.

Lambda: the eleventh letter of the Greek alphabet; in the Greek counting system it signifies the number 30.

Bibliography

Arianrhod, Robyn. 2011. *Seduced by Logic: Émilie du Châtelet, Mary Somerville and the Newtonian Revolution*. St Lucia: University of Queensland Press.

Banti, Anna. 1995. *Artemisia*. London: Serpent's Tail.

Barnard, Mary. 1958. *Sappho*. Berkeley: University of California Press.

Barnstone, Aliki and Willis Barnstone (eds). 1987. *A Book of Women Poets from Antiquity to Now*. New York: Schocken Books.

Barry, Kathleen. 1988. *Susan B. Anthony: The Biography of a Singular Feminist*. New York: New York University Press.

Beard, Mary. 2013. *Confronting the Classics: Traditions, Adventures and Innovations*. London: Profile Books.

Beard, Mary. 2008. *Pompeii: The Life of a Roman Town*. London: Profile Books.

Bellamy, Suzanne. 2005. 'Observing and Documenting the Transit of Patriarchy.' <http://www.suzannebellamy.com/pages/gallery3.html>.

Bellamy, Suzanne. 2009. 'Buried Women's Army as Part of The Steps Project.' <http://www.suzannebellamy.com/pages/gallery3.html>.

Bellamy, Suzanne. 2014. 'The Lost Culture of Women's Liberation: The Pre-Dynastic Phase, 1969–1974.' <http://youtu.be/hweqGjKq_es>.

Benedict XVI. ND. *The Apse Mosaic, Basilica di San Clemente*. San Francisco: Ignatius Press.

Betts, Gavin and David Franklin. 2007. *Beginning Latin Poetry Reader*. New York: McGraw Hill.

Biaggi, Cristina. 1994. *Habitations of the Great Goddess*. Manchester, Conn.: Knowledge, Ideas and Trends.

Brownfoot, Janice. 1983. 'Goldstein, Vida Jane (1869–1949).' *Australian Dictionary of Biography*, Vol. 9. Melbourne: Melbourne University Press. <http://adb.anu.edu.au/biography/goldstein-vida-jane-6418>.

Bumpass, Kathryn L. 1998. 'A Musical Reading of Hildegard's Responsory

"Spiritui Sancto".' In McInerney, Maud Burnett (ed.). *Hildegard of Bingen: A Book of Essays*. New York: Garland Publishing.

Carletti, Sandro. 2007. *Guide to the Catacombs of Priscilla*. Trans. Alice Mulhern. Vatican City: Pontifical Commission for Sacred Archaeology.

Carson, Anne. 2002. *If Not, Winter: Fragments of Sappho*. New York: Vintage.

Cataldi, Lee. 1978. *Invitation to a Marxist Lesbian Party*. Sydney: Wild and Woolley.

Curatrix, Xenia. 1978. 'Who invented Sulpicia? New works by women poets.' *Women's Studies International Forum*. Vol. 1, No. 1. pp. 29–33.

Curatrix, Xenia. 2013. 'slut but but.' YouTube. <http://www.youtube.com/watch?v=niXpHS9RU8k>

Daly, Mary. 1984. *Pure Lust: Elemental Feminist Philosophy*. San Francisco: HarperSanFrancisco. pp. 232–253.

Daly, Mary. 1998. *Quintessence … Realizing the Archaic Future: A Radical Elemental Feminist Manifesto*. Boston: Beacon Press.

Dashu, Max. 2013a. Suppressed History Archives. <http://www.suppressedhistories.net/secrethistory/oldgoddess.html>. Accessed 24 November 2013.

Dashu, Max. 2013b. Suppressed History Archives. <http://www.suppressedhistories.net/>. Accessed 20 December 2013.

Day, Jo. 2005. 'Adventures in Fields of Flowers: Research on Contemporary Saffron Cultivation and its Application to the Bronze Age Aegean.' In *SOMA 2003: Symposium of Mediterranean Archaeology*. Camilla Briault, Jack Green, Anthi Kaldelis, and Anna Stellatou. (eds). Oxford: Archeopress BAR S1391.

Day, Jo. 2011. 'Counting threads. Saffron in Aegean Bronze Age Writing and Society.' *Oxford Journal of Archaeology* 30(4): pp. 369–391.

Dexter, Miriam Robbins. 1990. *Whence the Goddesses: A Source Book*. New York: Pergamon Press (Athene Series).

di Prima, Diane. 1978. *Loba*. San Francisco: Wingbow Press.

Dickinson, Emily. 1961. *Final Harvest: Emily Dickinson's Poems*. (Thomas H. Johnson, ed.). Boston: Little Brown.

Ennius, Quintus. 2007. 'The Dream of Ilia.' Annales I fr. xxix. In Betts,

Gavin and David Franklin (eds). *Beginning Latin Poetry Reader*. New York: McGraw Hill. pp. 3–5.

Etruscan dictionary. 2013. <http://users.cwnet.com/millenia/ETRUSCANDICTIONARY.htm>. Accessed 22 August 2013.

Evelyn-White, Hugh G. (ed.). 2013. *Homer and Hesiod: The Homeric Hymns, and Homerica*. Project Gutenberg.

Fonseca, Lariane. 1992. *If Passion Were a Flower …* Melbourne: Spinifex Press.

Freisenbruch, Annelise. 2011. *The First Ladies of Rome: The Women behind the Caesars*. London: Vintage.

Gimbutas, Marija. 1989. *The Language of the Goddess*. San Francisco: Harper & Row.

Gimbutas, Marija. 1992. *The Civilization of the Goddess: The World of Old Europe*. San Francisco: HarperSanFrancisco.

Grahn, Judy. 1982. *The Queen of Swords*. Boston: Beacon Press.

Grant, Michael. 1971. *Roman Myths*. London: Weidenfeld and Nicolson.

Harrison, Barbara Grizzuti. 1989. *Italian Days*. New York: Atlantic Monthly Press.

Harrison, Jane Ellen. 1903/1980. *Prolegomena to the Study of Greek Religion*. London: Merlin Press.

Harrison, Jane Ellen. 1912/1977. *Themis: A Study of the Social Origins of Greek Religion*. Cambridge: The University Press.

Harrison, Jane Ellen. 1913. *Ancient Art and Ritual*. Oxford: Oxford University Press.

Harrison, Jane Ellen. 1921. *Epilegomena to the Study of Greek Religion*. Cambridge: The University Press.

Harrison, Jane Ellen. 1924. *Mythology*. New York: Harcourt Brace & World.

Hawthorne, Susan. 2011. 'Twenty verses from Meghadūta.' *Mascara Review*. <http://mascarareview.com/susan-hawthorne-translates-kalidasas-meghaduta/>.

Hawthorne, Susan. 2014. 'La Donna Lupa Paleolitica.' <http://susanslambdawolfblog.blogspot.it/2014/01/la-donna-lupa-paleolitica.html>.

Hildegard, Saint. 1994. *The Letters of Hildegard of Bingen*. Trans. Joseph L. Baird and Radd K. Ehrman. 2 Vols. Oxford: Oxford University Press.

Ilyatjari, Nganyintja. 1983. 'Women and Land Rights: Pitjantjatjara Land Claims.' In Fay Gale (ed.) *We are Bosses Ourselves: The Status and Role of Aboriginal Women Today*. Canberra: Australian Institute of Aboriginal Studies.

Jackson, Donna. 1997. 'Car Maintenance, Explosives and Love.' In Cathie Dunsford, Susan Hawthorne and Susan Sayer (eds). *Car Maintenance, Explosives and Love and Other Contemporary Lesbian Writings*. Melbourne: Spinifex Press. pp. 65–98.

Johnston, Jill and Marella Carracciolo Chia. 2010. *Niki de Saint Phalle and the Tarot Garden*. Photographs by Giulio Pietromarchi. Bern: Benteli.

La Barbe Groupe d'Action Féministe. <http://www.labarbelabarbe.org/La_Barbe/Accueil.html>.

La Gazzetta del Mezzogiorno. 2011. 'Ancient Etruscan "holy site" Found near Viterbo.' 26 July. <http://www.lagazzettadelmezzogiorno.it/english/ancient-etruscan-holy-site-found-near-viterbo-no444378/>.

La Lupa Capitolina. 2000. Rome: Electa.

Lambda-CDM model. 2013. <http://en.wikipedia.org/wiki/Lambda-CDM_model>. Accessed 15 September 2013.

Lessing, Doris. 1976. *The Golden Notebook*. St Albans: Granada Publishing.

Lessing, Doris. 1971. *Briefing for a Descent into Hell*. London: Jonathan Cape.

Livy. ND. *The History of Rome* 1.9. (Roberts). <http://www.class.uh.edu/mcl/classics/rom/livy.html>.

Marinatos, Nanno. 1984. *Art and Religion in Thera*. Athens: Mathioulakis.

Marinatos, Spyridon. 1976. *Excavations at Thera VII*. Athens. Standardized text from <http://www.minoanatlantis.com/End_Minoan_Writing.php>.

Melis, Paolo. 2003. *The Nuragic Civilization*. Sassari: Carlo Delfino editore.

Miller, Barbara Stoler. (ed.). 1984. *Theater of Memory: The Plays of Kālidāsa*. New York: Columbia University Press.

Moeller, Walter O. 1976. *The Wool Trade of Ancient Pompeii*. Leiden: Brill.

Moorhead, Finola. 2010. *Remember the Tarantella*. Melbourne: Spinifex Press.

Morgan, Robin. 1972. *Monster*. Melbourne: Radicalesbians. pp. 81–86.

Ovid. 2001. *Book 1 Amores* 'Elegy XIII The Dawn' lines 35–42. Trans. Kline, A.S. eBook.

Pope John. (numbering). 2014. <http://en.wikipedia.org/wiki/Pope_John_(numbering)>. Accessed 27 April 2014.

Powell, Eric A. 2014. 'Telling Tales in Proto-Indo-European.' *Archaeology*. <http://archaeology.org/exclusives/articles/1302-proto-indo-european-schleichers-fable>.

Rayor, Diane. 2004. *The Homeric Hymns*. Berkeley and Los Angeles: University of California Press.

Robinson, J. Armitage. 1891. *The Passion of S. Perpetua*. Cambridge: Cambridge University Press. <http://www.earlychurchtexts.com/main/perpetua/passio_of_perpetua_06.shtml>.

Rowley, Hazel. 2010. *Franklin and Eleanor: An Extraordinary Marriage*. Farrar, Straus and Giroux.

Russ, Joanna. 1983. *How to Suppress Women's Writing*. Austin: University of Texas Press.

Santoro, Suzanne. 1974. *Per una esspressione nuova / Towards a new expression*. Rome.

Settis, Salvatore. 2013. *La villa di Livia: Le pareti ingannevoli*. Rome: Electa.

Stack Exchange. 2014. 'Mathematics.' <http://math.stackexchange.com/questions/684089/meaning-of-variables-and-applications-in-lambda-calculus>.

Sulpicia, 'Epistulae.' <http://www.thelatinlibrary.com/sulpicia.html>.

Thadani, Giti. 1996. *Sakhiyani: Lesbian Desire in Ancient and Modern India*. London and New York: Cassell.

Thadani, Giti. 2004. *Moebius Trip*. Melbourne: Spinifex Press.

van der Meer, Annine. 2013. *The Language of MA the Primal Mother: The Evolution of the Female Image in 40,000 Years of Global Venus Art*. The Netherlands.

Waldman, Katy. 2014. 'Read Two Newly Discovered Sappho Poems in English for the First Time.' *Slate*. 31 January. <http://www.slate.com/blogs/browbeat/2014/01/31/read_two_newly_disc overed_sappho_poems_in_english_for_the_first_time.html>.

Wasson, R. Gordon, Albert Hofmann and Carl A.P. Ruck. 1978. *The Road to Eleusis: Unveiling the Secret of the Mysteries*. New York: Harcourt Brace Jovanovich.

Watson, Lilla. 1984. 'Aboriginal Women and Feminism.' Keynote Speech delivered at the Fourth Women and Labour Conference. Brisbane. July.

West, Martin. 2005. 'A New Sappho Poem.' *Times Literary Supplement*. 21 June. <http://www1.union.edu/wareht/story.html>.

Wittig, Monique. 1972. *The Guérillères*. London: Picador.

Wittig, Monique. 1987. *Across the Acheron*. London: Peter Owen.

Woolf, Virginia. 1976. 'A Sketch of the Past.' *Moments of Being: Unpublished Autobiographical Writings*. New York: Harcourt Brace Jovanovich.

Woolner, Alfred C. 1928/2008. *Introduction to Prakrit*. Delhi: Motilal Banarsidass.

Younger, J. 2013. 'Linear A at Haghia Triadha.' <http://archaeology.about.com/od/lterms/qt/linear_a.htm>. Accessed 22 August 2013.

Acknowledgements

My thanks to Lorri Whiting and the Australia Council whose support with a six-month Residency at the BR Whiting Library in Rome made this book possible. Along with the residency came a library of books, some of which have made it into this collection of poems. My thanks also to all connected to the Australia Council and to Pepita Andreas and Mariana Cofariu who worked magic with the plumbers. I also extend my thanks to the Australian embassies to Rome and the Holy See.

My time in Italy was made interesting and more understandable through those who have helped with languages, in particular Filoumina Anzivino at the DILIT School of Languages in Rome and Cristoforo Perino at the Centre for Italian Studies in Melbourne. The poets of Isola di Tiburina welcomed my halting readings and Claudia Perin provided remarkable instant translations and friendship. Marina Morbiducci invited me to talk to her students at the University of Sapienza and shares my excitement about translation.

Damjian Krsmanovic at the University of Melbourne introduced me to many literary Latin gems, as well as testing my grammatical limits. I continue to be grateful to those who have taught me Ancient Greek and Sanskrit.

In my second month in Rome I was lucky enough to travel to Torino for the Coffee Break Conference with scholars of Sanskrit and Asian Studies who in different ways opened new doors for me. Particular thanks to Elisa Freschi and Barbara Benedetti.

US-Italian artist, Suzanne Santoro befriended me on Facebook and we met in Rome early on. My heartfelt thanks, not only for lively conversation and feminist histories, but also for showing me parts of Rome I would not have known existed. Thank you for Capri and art.

Friends, Hilke Schlaeger and Gerlinde Kowitzke not only invited me to stay, but also took me to the Etruscan Necropoli in Tarquinia and the Giardino del Tarocchi, both of which have proved inspirational. Thanks to Rosanna Fiocchetto for telling me about La Donna Lupa Paleolitica. In my last week in Rome I made a special visit to Ancona to see her for myself. Annette Blight and Krista Bell included me in two tours in Rome and introduced me to several wonderful restaurants. Powhiri Wharemarama Kamira Rika-Heke's poetic distractions gave me renewed energy for the home run. There are friendships that span many years, women whose art and life have enriched me, among those who have followed this journey are Kaye Moseley, Suzanne Bellamy, Diane Bell, Meryl Waugh, Robin Arianrhod, Coleen Clare, Rye Senjen and Robin Morgan. Thanks to Meryl Waugh, for helping me unravel the complexities of astrophysics and Robyn Arianrhod for guiding me through the mathematics.

The women at Spinifex Press deserve enormous thanks, not only for letting me take off to Rome, but for all their energy in getting this book out. I am eternally grateful to Renate Klein for taking on my role at Spinifex along with Maralann Damiano, Pauline Hopkins, Helen Lobato, Bernadette Green, Danielle Binks and Jo O'Brien.

To all my endorsers, thank you for your words and enthusiasm and grazie mille to my Italian readers for spot checks of language and other matters. Any errors, of course, are my responsibility alone.

To Jordie Albiston, thank you for your inspirational editing. To Claire Warren, many thanks for the care with typesetting. To Pauline Hopkins for bilingual proofreading. To Deb Snibson, as always, thanks for the cover design. Also to Suzanne Bellamy for allowing me to use her Text Box image on the back cover, which was the inspiration for my Ooss poem; and to Renate Klein for the beautiful photo of Medusa, in the Gela Museum, Sicily, on the back cover.

Rome and love go hand in hand, and I cannot thank enough my partner, Renate Klein, who not only visited, and travelled to Sicily with me, but who also kept me up with news of home and provided a messaging service for our dog, Freya. I thank them for their love and patience during the period in which this book was being written and rewritten. Freya thanks her many mothers for pampering in my absence.

Some poems in this book have been previously published, often in different forms in the following publications: *PEN Newsletter*, *Rabbit*, *The Mago Circle*, *The Wonder Book of Poetry* and *Arc / Cordite*. Several poems have appeared on my blog: <http://susanslambdawolfblog.blogspot.com.au/>.

Other books by Susan Hawthorne

Cow

Shortlisted Kenneth Slessor Poetry Prize, NSW Premier's Literary Awards
Finalist Audre Lorde Lesbian Poetry Prize

> *Susan Hawthorne's writing is inventive, has fine use of allusions and metaphor and she challenges both the reader and herself to make old stories and commonplace creatures mean something new.*
>
> —Judges' citation, Kenneth Slessor Poetry Prize

> *I recommend you lie in bed and read it to your lover, or pleasure yourself with it, mouth it, tongue it, and maybe as I did, circle its words and metaphors, annotate, indulge in marginalia, dally in thesauri and etymologies and listen and be encouraged to sing along.*
>
> —Sarah St Vincent Welch, *Rochford Street Review*

Limen

When two women set off on a holiday they have no inkling of what's to come. They wake to find the river has crept up during the night. Trapped by floodwater, they devise escape routes only to be faced with new obstacles at every turn.

Only the dog remains calm.

> *The language is so spare, the line breaks so tight (on the back cover Robin Morgan compares the writing to haiku) that it makes the reader hold their breath. Reading this concentration of language is a little like river swimming, the glints of absolute certainty among the rocks and sand. Even without punctuation Hawthorne limits the breath, like that moment of stepping into deep water when the diaphragm flutters and adjusts.*
>
> —Lucy Alexander, *Verity La*

Earth's Breath

Shortlisted, Judith Wright Poetry Prize

Cyclonic storms inform the still eye of *Earth's Breath*. It's an eye that radiates with seismic intensity from personal to communal, from history to myth. In tracking her subject matter, Susan Hawthorne takes us from tranquillity to roar, bureaucratic inertia to survival, and the slow recovery from destruction to regeneration.

> Earth's Breath *builds like an exquisite thriller. Susan Hawthorne has told a story so vast that only a book of poetry could contain it.*
>
> —Kristin Henry, author *All the Way Home*

The Falling Woman

Top Twenty Title, *Listener* Women's Book Festival
Year's Best Books list, *The Australian*

A vivid desert journey; the falling woman travels through landscapes of memory, myth and mental maps. Told in three voices – Stella, Estella and Estelle – this is an inspiring story which weaves childhood, epilepsy, ancient mysteries and the love of two women.

> *This book commands endless reflection, since it opens up the ontological question of being. Hawthorne's book haunts me, it won't let go. On the one hand, it journeys through an unexplored territory of mind that few apart from Dostoyevski dared look into... Let me first say that this is a perfectly structured piece of writing. Its form should help unravel the threads of signification, but we are not dealing here with the explicit, let alone the assertive, or blatant.*
>
> —Jasna Novakovic, *Australian Women's Book Review*

If you would like to know more about Spinifex Press
write for a free catalogue or visit our website.

Spinifex Press
PO Box 212 North Melbourne
Vic 3051 Australia
www.spinifexpress.com.au